Sustainability of
Public Finances

Zentrum für Europäische Integrationsforschung (ZEI)
Center for European Integration Studies
University of Bonn

ZEI was established in 1995 as an applied research institute at the University of Bonn with the aim of bridging the gap between academia and public policy and business. Its three research groups in economics, political science and law focus on European affairs and policy questions and endeavour to contribute constructively to the resolution of the political, institutional and economic problems of European integration and Europe's long-term development. The research of ZEI's economics group emphasizes policy-oriented and empirical work, as well as political economy and macroeconomics.

ZEI hosts a number of economists, some of whom also hold academic positions at the University of Bonn and other universities, offering them a base for their research. ZEI collaborates with CEPR, NBER and other international research organizations. Through its regular workshops, conferences and informal meetings as well as through its research activities, ZEI also maintains active links to national and international policy institutions and the business community.

ZEI runs an active visitor's programme hosting a wide variety of researchers from around the world. Regular research seminars provide opportunities for visitors to present their work and discuss it with academic colleagues as well as policy-makers and decision-makers from the business world.

Zentrum für Europäische Integrationsforschung
Walter-Flex-Straße 3
D-53113 Bonn
Germany
Tel: (49) 228 739218   Fax: (49) 228 731809

Sustainability of Public Finances

Roberto Perotti
Columbia University and CEPR

Rolf Strauch
*Zentrum für Europäische Integrationsforschung,
University of Bonn*

Jürgen von Hagen
*Zentrum für Europäische Integrationsforschung,
University of Bonn, Indiana University and CEPR*

Zentrum für
Europäische
Integrations-
forschung

Centre for Economic Policy Research

The Centre for Economic Policy Research is a network of over 400 Research Fellows, based primarily in European universities. The Centre coordinates its Fellows' research activities and communicates their results to the public and private sectors. CEPR is an entrepreneur, developing research initiatives with the producers, consumers and sponsors of research. Established in 1983, CEPR is a European economics research organization with uniquely wide-ranging scope and activities.

CEPR is a registered educational charity. Institutional (core) finance for the Centre is provided by major grants from the Economic and Social Research Council, under which an ESRC Resource Centre operates within CEPR; the Esmée Fairbairn Charitable Trust; the Bank of England; the European Monetary Institute and the Bank for International Settlements; 22 national central banks and 40 companies. None of these organizations gives prior review to the Centre's publications, nor do they necessarily endorse the views expressed therein.

The Centre is pluralist and non-partisan, bringing economic research to bear on the analysis of medium- and long-run policy questions. CEPR research may include views on policy, but the Executive Committee of the Centre does not give prior review to its publications, and the Centre takes no institutional policy positions. The opinions expressed in this volume are those of the authors and not those of the Centre for Economic Policy Research.

20 February 1998

90–98 Goswell Road, London EC1V 7DB, UK
Tel: (44 171) 878 2900
Fax: (44 171) 878 2999
Email: cepr@cepr.org

British Library Cataloguing in Publication Data
A Catalogue record for this book is available from the British Library

ISBN 1 898128 35 9

Printed in Great Britain

Contents

List of Tables

List of Figures and Boxes

Executive summary

A basic tenet in the move to European Monetary Union (EMU) is that monetary stability requires the 'sustainability' of public finances. The Maastricht Treaty gives a dichotomous interpretation of sustainability: as long as a country meets the double standards of the *Excessive Deficit Procedure*, a general government budget deficit below 3% and a public debt below 60% of GDP, its public finances will be regarded 'sustainable', if it violates these criteria, they will not. The Treaty, however, gives no clear guidance for evaluating the public finances of a country violating these criteria, i.e. for judging whether or not it has taken adequate measures of adjustment, and whether or not it is moving in the right direction. These questions are also left open by the more recent *Stability and Growth Pact*. As the beginning of EMU draws nearer and almost all European Union countries violate the double standards, a more developed interpretation of sustainability is necessary to guide the judgements regarding a country's readiness for membership in EMU, and for a continuous monitoring of the members' public finances once EMU has started.

Developing a practical approach to assess the sustainability of a country's public finances is the purpose of this study. More precisely, we develop a framework for evaluating the process of regaining sustainability once it has been lost, since, following the logic of the Maastricht Treaty, no further assessment is necessary if the country meets the double standards.

Our approach rests on *four principles*:

■ a focus on controllability as the key issue;
■ the principle of attacking the problem at the source;

- the distinction between short-run symptoms and long-run sources of non-sustainable government public finances;

- the proposition that non-sustainable public finances ultimately result from institutional weaknesses.

Specifically, we argue that policy-makers are more worried about situations where governments lose control of spending and deficits, and are heading towards an unavoidable, disruptive adjustment of taxes and spending than about any particular level of public debts or deficits. It is precisely such adjustments that might cause difficulties for the conduct of monetary policy under EMU. Thus, our interpretation of sustainability focuses on the issue of control over government spending, revenues and the deficit, rather than a vague intertemporal budget constraint. The implication is that a sustainable deficit reduction is one in which the government reliably and lastingly regains control over its budget.

There is overwhelming empirical evidence showing that the lasting success of fiscal consolidations depends critically on following *the principle of attacking the problem at the source*. This principle has the following components:

- the origin of non-sustainable public finances can usually be traced back to one or two critical elements of the government budget, such as wage expenditures or transfers;

- successful, i.e. lasting fiscal consolidations come with a significant reduction in those elements that lead to the emergence of a fiscal problem in the first place.

The implication is that an assessment of the sustainability of a country's public finances requires a disaggregate view of its government budget. Looking just at aggregate spending, revenues and the deficit is clearly insufficient for making a valid assessment.

In view of this, it is important to identify the symptoms of non-sustainability properly: on which side of the budget did the deficit emerge and what were the more detailed budget items behind this development? The evidence we give in this study, both from statistical analyses and from a number of case studies, shows very clearly that successful consolidations are those that apply this principle and unsuccessful ones are those that do not.

Budget numbers can only be the symptoms of non-sustainable fiscal policies, however. Behind these numbers are the real causes of the problem. These causes can commonly be linked to weaknesses of a country's economic policy institutions. Most importantly, flaws in the decision-making rules and practices regarding public monies lead to the emergence of excessive spending and deficits. We consider two aspects of this:

- *fragmentation* of the budget process;
- the *spreading of non-decisions* coupled with weaknesses in other economic policy institutions.

Fragmentation of the budget process occurs when representatives of particular spending interests in society are allowed to make spending decisions without taking the full cost of public policy programmes into consideration. It is due to the common characteristic of modern public finance that spending programmes are more narrowly targeted at specific groups in society than taxation. A growing body of empirical literature, including statistical tests as well as case studies, and considering very different countries, shows that fragmentation is an important source of excessive government deficits.

Fragmentation can be overcome by strengthening rules and institutions of the budget process that force policy-makers to take a comprehensive view of the costs and benefits of public-policy programmes. There are two important approaches in practice:

- *delegation* of significant budgetary powers to a 'strong' finance minister; and
- *contracts focusing on spending and deficit targets* among the relevant decision-makers.

Empirical evidence shows that both approaches help governments maintain sustainable public finances. This implies that institutional reforms of the budget process are an important element of an effort to regain sustainability of a country's public finances. The Maastricht Treaty recognizes this by demanding that the EMU member states implement budget processes enabling them to maintain sustainable public finances (Art. 3 of the Protocol on the Excessive Deficit Procedure).

The choice between the two approaches, however, depends importantly on the political environment of a country, mainly its electoral system. The theory and evidence both indicate that the reason why the Maastricht process of fiscal convergence failed to achieve general fiscal discipline in all EMU countries is precisely because its central elements, fiscal targets enforced through external monitoring and control, are inadequate institutional mechanisms for the large countries of the EMU.

Non-decisions occur in the budget process when governments leave the determination of spending and deficits to variables outside their direct control. Examples are the indexation of spending programmes and fixing the parameters of entitlements by laws outside the budget process. Non-decisions reduce the budget process to a mere forecasting exercise of exogenous events, while allowing policy-makers to avoid tough decisions that might be unpopular with their constituencies. Importantly in our context, non-decisions make the controllability of the budget depend on the qualities of institutions outside the annual budget process, e.g. labour market or welfare institutions. The implication is that, where non-decisions cannot be eliminated, the reform of other economic policy institutions can become an important element of the process of regaining sustainability of a country's public finances. The European Council has recently recognized this principle by asking the Italian government to undertake a reform of the Italian pension system as a condition for entering EMU.

In summary, we conclude that *institutional reforms are an important part of a country's effort to regain sustainability, and that governments can and should be asked to undertake such reforms when they have violated the double standards.*

How should an assessment of a country's public finances proceed on this basis? To answer this question, we develop a process of *five stages*, starting after a violation of the double standards:

Stage 0: Does the country show a sufficient change of the deficit in the right direction, where *sufficient* means at least one-half of one per cent of GDP? If not, the country remains at stage 0.

Stage 1: A sufficient move in the right direction has occurred. Next we consider the contribution of spending and revenues to the deficit and apply the *two-thirds rule*: Has the country reduced the ratio of spending (revenues) to GDP by at least two thirds of the increase (decline) it experienced in the years when the deficit emerged?

Stage 2: Sufficient action on the right side of the budget has been taken. Next we disaggregate spending (revenues): Has the country reduced (reversed the decline of) the principal elements of spending (revenues) that lead to the growth of spending (decline in revenues) during the emergence of the deficit?

Stage 3: Sufficient action has been taken to address the symptoms of the deficit. Now we turn to the institutional sources. Has the government identified the institutional weaknesses leading to the emergence of the deficit and addressed them informally?

Stage 4: The underlying weaknesses have been identified. The last question remains: Has the government engaged in institutional reforms to overcome these weaknesses?

These stages are not to be seen necessarily as following each other strictly over time; rather, they mark qualitative stages of the process. The questions at stages 0, 1 and 2 are straightforward to answer on the basis of budgetary statistics. The questions at stages 3 and 4 are more difficult to assess and rely on more qualitative information. Answering them, therefore, leads to more contentious debate. *Realizing this, we advocate that a country should not be declared having regained sustainability unless it passes stage 2 successfully.* Realistically, the answers to the questions at stages 3 and 4 should be used to qualify the evidence regarding the symptoms and make more informed judgements about them.

Applying this procedure does not result in a tightening of the Excessive Deficit Procedure or the Stability and Growth Pact; instead, it provides a broader and more qualitative approach than the mere focus on aggregate budget numbers under the latter. *The keys to sustainability are thus a disaggregate view of the budget and a close scrutiny of institutions.*

Following traditions of the European Community, one may of course argue that the EMU has no business interfering with the structure of a member country's public finances, and much less with its economic policy institutions. However, this tradition will have to cede with EMU: if one believes that sustainability is an important condition for the success of EMU, one must accept that the EMU has a rightful interest in monitoring the fiscal policies of the member states at a deeper level than just the aggregate deficit, and to demand structural and institutional adjustments where necessary.

1

Sustainability of public finances

A basic assumption in the move to European Monetary Union (EMU) is that monetary stability requires the stability of public finances. The idea that mounting public debts would undermine the European Central Bank's ability to fulfil its mandate of price stability runs through all important documents and decisions marking the way to EMU, from the Delors Report (1989) to the Maastricht Treaty (1991), and the Stability and Growth Pact of the Treaty of Amsterdam (1997), and has been a recurrent theme in the public debate over EMU. It is grounded in gruesome historical experience – most notably, perhaps, the German hyperinflation of the early 1920s and the German currency reform of 1948 – as well as technical economic analysis, e.g. the *monetarist arithmetic* of Sargent and Wallace (1981).

Specifically, the Maastricht Treaty (Art. 109j(1)) makes the 'sustainability of the government's financial position' an explicit criterion for a country's eligibility for EMU. However, while there is widespread agreement over the basic issue – the close link between monetary and government financial stability – there is no consensus about the proper definition of sustainability. The Maastricht Treaty (Art. 109j) refers to the two critical reference values of the Excessive Deficit Procedure defined in Art. 104c and the relevant Protocol, namely a public sector deficit not exceeding 3% and a public sector debt not exceeding 60% of GDP. If all member states of the EMU aspiring to join EMU met these criteria, no further debate would be necessary about sustainability in practice. Given that they do not, a practical definition will have to be found for the final evaluation of the candidates for EMU, and for the continued assessment of their fiscal performance once EMU has started.

Although on paper the Treaty regulations regarding fiscal policy appear fairly specific, the political reality is such that in practice they allow a considerable degree of elasticity in their interpretation. Thus, as the deadline for EMU membership approaches, policy-makers are facing two kinds of problems. The more immediate one is to develop and agree on a framework for evaluating the fiscal policy of a country in deciding about membership in EMU. The longer-term problem is how to develop a framework for monitoring the public finances of those countries that have become members.

1.1 Sustainability: the problem and a pragmatic framework

Controllability of public finances is the key issue for the stability of a common currency.

What, then, is *sustainability*? The Maastricht Treaty does not qualify the notion of sustainability beyond the two criteria, and therefore provides no guidance for evaluating the policies of a country violating them.

For the economist, sustainability is a forward-looking concept, requiring that current and expected future government revenues and expenditures match in a present-value sense. For practical purposes, this notion of sustainability is quite useless, as it does not sufficiently constrain current government policies – anything can be assumed about the future.

In this paper, we adopt a more pragmatic approach. We take it as given that, for a number of economic and political reasons, membership in the EMU will entail some form of controls on the fiscal policy of a member country, and we do not discuss the desirability of such controls as a matter of principle. Instead, we ask two closely related questions:

■ What aspects of fiscal policy are most relevant for the stability of a common currency?

■ How does the answer to the first question translate into feasible constraints on the public finances of a country seeking membership or being a member of EMU?

In answering these two questions, we argue that the *controllability* of public finances is the key issue for the stability of a common currency. Policy-makers, and central bankers in particular, worry more about the risk that a government's financial position is moving out of their hands than about any particular level of deficits and debts. According to this view, the important issue is to avoid situations in which a government, for some reason or other, has lost control over the public sector deficit and is heading towards an unavoidable and disruptive adjustment. Such situations would cause interest rates to rise steeply and force the government to undertake large and disruptive changes in spending and taxation. Large increases in interest rates that may spread across borders within the EMU, and large swings in the budgetary position of a government create much more severe problems for the conduct of EMU monetary policy than a high, but stable debt ratio. This view lurks behind the Maastricht Treaty's mandate for the European Commission to monitor the fiscal performance of the member states in order to 'identify gross errors' (Art. 104c(2)).

Thus, we propose to shift the focus of *sustainability* to the more practical issue of *controllability*. An immediate implication of this view is that a *sustainable deficit reduction* should be regarded as a fiscal policy adjustment assuring, with reasonable certainty, that the government has indeed regained control over its financial position. We will argue below that controllability can be reasonably assessed on the basis of current and past data, which makes the concept more adequate for practical policy.

A sustainable deficit reduction should assure that the government has indeed regained control over its financial situation.

In developing a definition of sustainability based on controllability, we try to concentrate on *feasible* criteria and restrictions. The emphasis on *feasibility* reflects our conviction that the specific form of the restrictions on the fiscal policy of the member countries should take political and informational constraints into consideration. It is of no use to advocate a restriction that cannot be enforced – be it because it is politically unacceptable for sovereign countries, because it requires too much detailed information, or because it involves too much subjectivity. Our guiding principle, therefore, will be the realism of the analysis and the practical applicability of our conclusions.

As noted above, the Maastricht Treaty, in developing a definition of sustainability, takes a dichotomous approach. As long as a country meets the double standards, the sustainability of its public finances is assumed by the EMU as a matter of principle. There is no need for a detailed assessment of its public finances in that case. A practical assessment of sustainability matters only in the opposite case, when the country violates the double standards. Below, we follow the same logic. We do not intend to construct a measure of sustainability to be used in all possible situations. Instead, we propose a set of criteria to evaluate and guide a country through the process of regaining sustainability once the benign presumption has been violated.

In the next sections we elaborate on these notions and develop the answers to the two basic questions.

1.2 Sustainability and the intertemporal budget constraint

In answering the two questions above, it is useful to start by reviewing the rationale for the fiscal criteria of the Maastricht Treaty. These criteria rest on three basic premises:

1. Large and persistent budget deficits eventually generate pressure on monetary authorities to bail out the fiscal authorities.

2. In a common currency area with high capital mobility, developments in capital markets in one country will affect interest rates in all other countries.

3. At high levels of debt, a country is increasingly vulnerable to confidence and financial crises as the market starts fearing some form of default on the debt. The resulting default risk premium on the country's interest rate will spread to the other member countries as the market assumes that some bail out will occur in case of a crisis.

These three types of concerns underlie the two main fiscal criteria in the Maastricht Treaty, the 3% deficit rule and the 60% debt rule. Economists have long pointed out that the economic rationale for these specific numerical criteria is questionable.[1] The academic discussion of sustainability has focused instead on the concept of an intertemporal budget constraint.

In the most general sense, the intertemporal government budget constraint requires that the discounted sum of expected future tax revenues is enough to repay all present (the current debt) and future (the discounted sum of all expected future expenditures) liabilities of the government. To assess whether or not a government would meet its intertemporal budget constraint given its current debt, revenues and expenditures, one has to form expectations about the future time-paths of revenues and expenditures.

This approach has two obvious problems. First, it is very sensitive to assumptions about future interest rates and growth rates of GDP. Since the assessment involves cumulating expected future budget surpluses over an infinite horizon, even small changes in the difference between predicted interest rate and GDP growth can lead to very different conclusions about sustainability. Second, because forecasts of future revenues and expenditures in practice extrapolate from the past, they are likely to miss recent changes in fiscal policy. Suppose that a government has drastically reduced expenditures in the last two or three years through a structural reform that promises to be permanent. Assuming that it is permanent, the new stance of fiscal policy should be used to forecast future developments. This recent change, however, will have little impact on an empirical assessment which would necessarily be based on observations from a longer history. The reform, therefore, would receive unduly little weight in the assessment of sustainability.

To overcome these problems, Blanchard *et al.* (1990) propose a modified concept of sustainability. According to their definition, a government's fiscal policy is *sustainable* over a horizon of *n* years if it leaves the government debt to GDP ratio unchanged over this time horizon, or, more generally, if the ratio is the same in the first and the last year of the period considered. One practical implementation of the concept consists in calculating the constant budget surplus that would ensure that *n* years from now the debt will be stable at a given level. The difference between the current and this constant *sustainable* surplus then indicates the current fiscal stance: it is sustainable, if the former is at least as large as the latter. In this rendition, the empirical assessment of sustainability still suffers from the first problem pointed out above, but not from the second.

Brandner, Diebalek and Schuberth (1997) try to avoid even the first problem. They apply a univariate time-series technique[2] to compute the trend component of public resource flows. The authors interpret this trend component as the structural element of the budget. This allows them to derive a structural primary budget balance without recurrence to questionable assumptions concerning elasticities of the budget with regard to real income and the interest rate. Then, they compare the actual budget balance with the structural balance needed to stabilize the debt level. According to this procedure, a country's public finances are sustainable if the former exceeds the latter. Although this empirically oriented approach seems to avoid debatable assumptions about economic parameters, it actually does not solve the problem. Rather, the focus shifts towards the selection of econometric techniques and the determination of estimation parameters.[3]

Conventional concepts of sustainability are highly sensitive to assumptions about the future.

Thus, any conclusion based on these forward-looking concepts of sustainability is highly sensitive to assumptions about the future interest rates, GDP growth, developments in the demographic structure of the population or the applied technique. This is a rather shaky basis for important political decisions; it invites endless debates over the appropriateness of every single assumption and forecast. Such debates would be perfectly justifiable – judging from the ex-post accuracy of just two-years-ahead forecasts of real growth and interest rates presented by international organizations, it would take an inordinate amount of faith to base any important decision on the medium-term projections of the type involved in estimating sustainability in this way.

It is simply not realistic to assume that such calculations guide policy decisions as important as EMU membership or the invocation of the Excessive Deficit Procedure. Nor is it realistic to believe that an agreement could be reached on this basis in an international body such as the European Council. Policy-makers judging the adequacy of a country's fiscal policy for the common currency area will want to base their decisions on unambiguous, easily available numbers and avoid difficult forecasts of the future. In this study, we argue that such a measure can be constructed and, what is more, that it is much more likely to capture those aspects of fiscal policy that concern policy-makers most.

1.3 The solution: focusing on controllability

Although the effects of debts and deficits on interest rates and on monetary stability – which as we have seen motivate the fiscal criteria of the Maastricht Treaty – are long-standing and highly controversial issues, here too we do not enter the debate but rather take a pragmatic approach. In answering the first question asked above, 'What aspects of fiscal policy are most relevant for the stability of a common currency?' we recognize that, for whatever reason, both the market and policy-makers do worry about the possibility of fiscal policy jeopardizing the stability of a common currency area.

We argue, however, that what they worry about is mostly the possibility that a government might lose control over the *deficit* for a period of time and that this would pose difficult problems for the monetary policy in the EMU. The ensuing increase in interest rates or, more seriously, a financial crisis might spread to all member countries. The government might be forced to adopt drastic measures of adjustment, with macroeconomic effects that, again, might spread across other EMU economies. Both developments would result in public demands for a more lenient monetary policy, and compromise the European Central Bank's ability and willingness to pursue a strict policy of price stability.

Two examples are instructive. In 1994, with a large deficit and no clear policy strategy for reducing it, a default by the Italian government on its public debt was considered by many as a real possibility. In 1997, after just two years of relatively strict fiscal policies that have reduced the deficit substantially, few would cite a default on the public debt as a major concern. Yet, the debt to GDP ratio has barely been stabilized. Thus, to a large extent what really matters for the market's assessment of Italy's fiscal policy is the expected flow of government (net) liabilities in the next few years, not the stock.[4]

Germany provides the other example. Since the unification of Germany in 1990, the Bundesbank has warned repeatedly that the federal government's fiscal performance was becoming increasingly non-sustainable. This criticism was clearly not directed at Germany's debt ratio, which remains relatively low in a European comparison. Instead, it was the government's policy of responding to the mounting difficulties of reconstructing East Germany by simply increasing subsidies and transfers that caused the central bank to worry. The impression that the government had lost the political will to contain the mounting demands for subsidies and, hence, control over the fiscal flows seems to have played a much bigger role than the stock of public debt in itself.

Hence, from the central bankers' and the markets' point of view, the crucial issue in sustainability ultimately is the *controllability* of fiscal policy. Broadly speaking, controllability regards the risk that a bad shock affecting revenues or its spending commitments leaves a government unable, technically or politically, to prevent spending and deficits from growing beyond their desirable and economically justifiable levels for a prolonged period of time.

From the central bankers' and the markets' point of view, the crucial issue is the controllability of fiscal policy.

1.4 Securing sustainability: attacking the problem at the source

Controllability of public finances should be based on the principle of attacking the problem at the source.

Having provided a definition of sustainability in terms of controllability, we now turn to the second question – what type of restrictions best ensure the sustainability (controllability) of fiscal policy? As we have argued above, controllability of fiscal policy has inherently much more to do with the flow of government net liabilities than with the stock of debt. The focus, therefore, should be on fiscal flows rather than stocks.

Of course, the stock of debt can affect the flow, which is probably the reason for the 60% debt ratio in the Maastricht Treaty. One way this can happen is that an exogenous increase in interest rates leads to higher interest payments and, particularly in countries with high levels of debt, to a larger deficit. Again, however, the focus is ultimately on the flow, not on the level of the debt *per se*.

The Maastricht Treaty's limit on the deficit ratio correctly turns attention to the flows, but even the tighter version agreed upon in the Stability and Growth Pact – a deficit of 1% in normal times – does not provide a sufficient assurance of what really matters, namely controllability. The reason is that the aggregate deficit alone tells us little about whether or not a government is willing and able to rectify the problem permanently, once its public finances have gone out of control.

An example will best illustrate our position. Suppose that the deadline for admission to EMU is year T, and in year $T-2$ a country still has a large deficit, in the order of 10% of GDP. This deficit had mushroomed in the five years before $T-2$, caused mainly by a loss of control over the wage bill at the local level and by exploding transfer expenditures. Suppose also that, through a major revenue-raising effort, the country manages to satisfy the 3% limit on the deficit by year T. However, nothing has been done on the two sources of the deficit. In this situation, the mere fulfilment of the 3% rule says little about the controllability of fiscal policy, because, with no measures on the underlying causes, we should expect wages and transfers to continue to rise and the deficit to reappear after a while. As long as the government fails to address the causes of the problem, the deficit is virtually guaranteed to get out of control again.

The implication is that a measure designed to monitor and enforce the controllability of public finances should be based on the *principle of attacking the problem at the source*: to judge the sustainability of a country's public finances, not only the size of the deficit is important, but also knowing what caused it and what the country has done to correct it.

By their nature, the criteria in the Maastricht Treaty, which set limits on aggregate magnitudes only, cannot embody the principle of attacking the problem at the source. Devising feasible criteria that do the job is not easy. On the one hand, the principle calls for more specific information and restrictions than the 3% deficit rule. On the other hand, it would be unrealistic to try to regulate too finely how a sovereign country should run its fiscal policy.

As a first step towards a realistic solution, it is helpful to distinguish between the symptoms and sources of a loss of sustainability. Symptoms can be recognized and attacked in the short run, while the underlying sources of the problem will often need a longer time horizon to be addressed properly. To some extent, the same difference in perspective also characterizes the decisions about membership and the evaluation of the performance of member countries in the common currency area.

1.5 Monitoring sustainability: symptoms and sources

In the short run, the first need is a readily available and uncontroversial measure that raises a red flag as soon as a problem develops. Naturally, such a measure is likely to focus more on the *symptoms* of a loss of sustainability than on the true sources of the problem. In the longer run, it is important also to be able to detect the underlying *sources* of the lack of sustainability. This leads us to the distinction between *functional* and *institutional* aspects of non-sustainability. Loosely speaking, this distinction corresponds to that between *symptoms* and *sources* of non-sustainability.

Loosely speaking, the distinction between functional and institutional aspects of non-sustainability corresponds to that between symptoms and sources.

1.5.1 Detecting symptoms: disaggregating spending and taxation

Large increases in the deficit in the short run, can almost always be ascribed to a few specific budget items. For instance, the wage bill of local governments might suddenly start building up, due to a generous policy of public hiring or to generous wage settlements after a contentious round of negotiations with public sector unions. Alternatively, social transfers might increase strongly, due to a sudden change in the eligibility criteria, more generous replacement ratios in unemployment benefits and old-age pensions, changes in the indexation rules, etc.

In a sense, these are just *symptoms* of the loss of control over public finances. They are, however, easily detectable, with a minimal delay, and objectively measurable. Any good cure starts with a reliable detection of symptoms. A good short-run indicator of a government's loss of control over public finances should, therefore, provide information not only about the change in the aggregate deficit, but also about its main components. *Disaggregation* of government spending and taxation is thus an essential part of any good measure of sustainability. For this purpose, *numerical* indicators are useful, visible and uncontroversial, but they should be developed not just for the aggregate deficit, but also for the main components of government spending and revenues.

Disaggregation of government spending and taxation is an essential part of any good measure of sustainability.

The European Commission's (1997a) recent study of the 'Economic Policy Under EMU' correctly notes that disaggregation of the budget data is an important part of the evaluation of the sustainability of public finances. It is, however, only a first step in applying the principle of attacking the problem at the source. Beyond the description of a country's recent fiscal developments, the principle requires to take corrective action on those components where the budget problems emerged. The numerical indicator used to detect the symptoms of non-sustainability should, therefore, also provide the basis for judging the compliance with this principle. We propose such an indicator in Chapter 5.

1.5.2 Detecting sources: institutional deficiencies

Underlying these symptoms are the deeper sources of non-sustainable public finances. Our basic claim in this study is that problems with rising expenditures and deficits – the symptoms of non-sustainability – can generally be traced back to institutional deficiencies, i.e. weaknesses in the decision-making processes governing the government budget and the policies financed with public monies.

A first, important area where this claim applies is the government budget process. An increasing body of research in the political economy of public finances emphasizes the impact of the decision-making rules and practices regarding government expenditures and revenues on the size of the budget and the budget deficit. In the examples above, the wage bill might have got out of control because of lack of control over the hiring decisions of local governments with no autonomous revenue-raising powers.

One important cause for rising expenditures and deficits according to this literature (e.g. Weingast *et al.*, 1981; von Hagen and Harden, 1996) is the tendency of policy-makers to pay more attention to the benefits of the spending programmes than the resulting need for increased revenues. As explained in Chapter 4, this tendency results from a general characteristic of modern public finances, *viz.* that spending programmes are generally targeted more narrowly at individual groups in society than the collection of revenues. The more *fragmented* decision-making processes over the budget are, i.e. the more decision-makers they involve and the more they allow each individual participant to get what he or she demands, the more this leads to overspending and large deficits.[5]

Political economy emphasizes the spreading of *non-decisions* as another, important source of a loss of control over the deficit. Government spending often increases, because the relevant expenditures are tied to entitlements or indexed to economic variables outside the direct control of the government. In many countries, welfare payments are a prime example for this. Once the basic parameters are fixed by law, government spending simply responds passively to the public's demand for transfers. Expenditures thus move outside the realm of the annual decision-making process over the public budget. In the context of the annual preparation of the budget, indexing spending programmes to the general price level is another example. Allowing policy-makers to avoid hard choices by referring difficult problems to informal decision-making bodies outside the regular process of public budgeting is a third version of the problem, e.g. the German government's practice to seek a compromise with the social partners over its labour market policies in the 1990s. In all these instances of *constitutional failure* (von Hagen and Harden, 1994), governments exploit weaknesses of the decision-making process to *avoid* control over certain aspects of fiscal policies.

These are the underlying *sources* of the loss of control over public finances. They are, however, more difficult to identify clearly, and obviously impossible to measure precisely. They are also likely to be much more contentious, and involve sensitive

In instances of constitutional failure, governments exploit weaknesses of the decision-making process to avoid control.

political and constitutional issues. Hence, indicators of problems in the institutional arrangements must necessarily be *qualitative*. In addition, changing institutional arrangements must be expected to take more time than a change in government spending and taxes, and this should be taken into account in a realistic judgement of sustainability.

Nevertheless, the Maastricht Treaty, in Article 3 of the Protocol on the Excessive Deficit Procedure, requires the EMU member states to ensure that their domestic decision-making processes over budgetary affairs enable them to fulfil their obligations and deliver stable and sustainable public finances. Furthermore, the European Council in July 1997 argued that Italy needed significant changes in the public pension system and the tax system to achieve a sustainable stance of its public finances and required adequate institutional reforms from the Italian government as a precondition to enter EMU. This indicates that the existence, and the creation of institutional arrangements conducive to sustainability can be included in a practical assessment of a country's public finances in EMU.

In the next two chapters, we present empirical evidence that strongly corroborates the importance of these two aspects of controllability and the importance of the principle of attacking the problem at the source to enforce sustainability. On the basis of this evidence and of our theoretical discussion so far, we put forth our specific proposals in Chapter 5 for a set of criteria to assess sustainability in practice.

2

Controllability and fiscal consolidation: evidence

In this chapter, we use government budget data of 20 OECD countries in the past 25 years to illustrate the importance of the principle of attacking the problem at the source.

2.1 Loss of control of the budget and composition

In Table 2.1, we study episodes of big fiscal expansions as examples of periods where governments lost control of their public finances. Specifically, we isolate all those years where the ratio of the cyclically-adjusted deficit to GDP increased by more than 1.5% and call them *big expansions*. In the sample of 20 OECD countries after 1973, there are 65 such episodes.

Table 2.1 Contributions to big fiscal expansions

	Contribution	T-statistic
Expenditures	69.9	12.1
Investment	3.6	1.9
Transfers	41.2	9.1
Consumption	19.9	6.9
Wage expenditures	14.0	6.0
Non-wage consumption	5.9	4.0
Subsidies	4.9	1.7
Revenues	−30.1	−5.2
Taxes on income	−11.2	−2.1
Taxes on business	−5.9	−3.5
Indirect taxes	−12.9	−3.4

Note: Number of observations: 65.

The table shows the average contribution to total increase in the deficit during big fiscal expansions of the increase in aggregate expenditure, the decline in revenues and of the individual budget items. This table drives home two points.

First, and perhaps not surprisingly, most of the increase in the deficit (70%) is due to increases in expenditures, against a fall in revenues by 30%. Second, almost all the increase in expenditures is due to two items: transfers and government consumption.

Most of the time very specific budget items are responsible for a loss of control over the budget.

Hence, this table supports very clearly the main premise of our approach, that most of the time very specific budget items are responsible for a loss of control over the budget.

2.2 Successful and unsuccessful consolidations

Next, in Table 2.2 we study different modes of consolidating the budget.[6] We study all those episodes where the cyclically-adjusted deficit falls by at least 1.5% of GDP. We call these episodes *consolidations*.

We then take all these episodes, and divide them into *successful* and *unsuccessful* consolidations. Success is defined in terms of persistence. Specifically, we define a consolidation successful, if either one or both of the following two conditions is realized: the deficit, as a share of GDP, does not increase in the two years after the consolidation; or the debt to GDP ratio falls by at least 3 percentage points in the two years after the consolidation. A consolidation is unsuccessful, if neither one of these conditions is realized.

Thus, only successful consolidations lead to a persistent reduction in the deficit. Unsuccessful consolidations are short-lived: the initial cut in the deficit cannot be maintained. Hence, one can interpret successful consolidations as those where the deficit is taken back under control for a prolonged period of time: in other words, successful consolidations embed our notion of sustainability.

Table 2.2 displays how much each budget item contributed, on average, to consolidations (column 1), to successful ones (column 2) and to unsuccessful ones (column 3). The table contains three very clear messages. First, the *size* of a typical successful consolidation is virtually the same as the size of a typical unsuccessful one: on average, the deficit ratio falls by 2.4% in the former and by 2.3% in the latter case. The *composition*

Table 2.2 Contributions to successful and unsuccessful consolidations

	All		Success		Failure	
	Contr.	T-stat.	Contr.	T-stat.	Contr.	T-stat.
No. of observations	47		19		28	
Deficit	−2.3		−2.4		−2.3	
Expenditures	−30.5	4.6	−50.2	−6.3	−17.1	−1.9
Investment	−12.1	−5.6	−13.3	−3.9	−11.2	−4.0
Transfers	−1.3	−0.4	−9.6	−2.8	4.3	1.0
Consumption	−10.8	−3.1	−18.9	3.2	−5.3	−1.3
Wage expenditures	−6.6	2.3	−14.5	−3.6	−1.2	−0.3
Non-wage consumption	−4.2	−3.5	−4.4	−1.9	−4.1	−3.2
Subsidies	−4.0	−1.9	−8.1	−3.1	−1.2	−0.4
Revenues	69.5	10.4	49.8	6.2	82.9	9.2
Taxes on income	36.6	5.4	21.3	2.4	47.0	5.1
Taxes on business	10.9	4.2	10.6	2.7	11.1	3.2
Indirect taxes	22.0	7.3	17.9	3.6	24.8	6.6

Note: Deficit as percentage of GDP. All others as percentage of consolidation.

of the adjustment is, however, drastically different in the two cases. In successful consolidations, expenditure cuts contribute 50% to the adjustment; in unsuccessful ones, expenditures cuts account for only 17% of the adjustment. Unsuccessful consolidations rely mainly on increased revenues. Thus, a decisive action to stop and reverse expenditure growth is a key element of successful consolidation.[7]

Decisive action to stop and reverse expenditure growth is a key element of successful consolidation.

The second message of Table 2.2 concerns the composition of the expenditure cuts. Within expenditures, two items make up most of the difference between successful and unsuccessful consolidations: transfers and wage expenditures. Cuts in transfers contribute 10% to the total adjustment during successful episodes, while during unsuccessful ones they actually increase! Even more starkly, cuts in wage expenditures contribute 14.5% to the fall in the deficit during successful consolidations, but little more than 1% to unsuccessful ones. Non-wage government expenditures and capital expenditures, by contrast, behave almost identically in the two types of consolidations.

The third point concerns the disaggregation of revenues. Not only do successful consolidations rely much less on revenue increases than unsuccessful ones; the composition of the change in revenues is also very different. Table 2.2 shows that virtually the entire difference on the revenue side between successful and unsuccessful consolidations is due to labour taxes (income taxes and social security taxes), which contribute 21% to the adjustment in the former and 47% to the adjustment in the latter case. This is important, because labour taxes are shifted on to wages. Particularly in small, open economies, a group to which most of the European countries belong, this causes drastic increases in labour costs relative to trading partners.

These messages of Table 2.2 are very robust to variations in the empirical method. Similar and, indeed, even stronger results can be obtain using alternative criteria.[8] Thus, one might vary the criterion of success, making it more or less stringent or looking further into the future than just two years. One might consider larger consolidations than those of 1.5% of GDP. One might use different data or different methodologies for seasonal adjustment. Despite some differences in the details, the basic message remains the same.[9]

In summary, Table 2.2 shows forcefully that not all consolidations are alike. They lead to a sustained improvement of the budget only if they avoid increasing labour taxes too much and if they tackle the growth of expenditures directly, particularly the rise in transfers and wage expenditures.

2.3   Attacking the problem at the source

Piecing Table 2.1 and Table 2.2 together already provides strong evidence in support of our principle of attacking the problem at the source. Table 2.1 shows that loss of control of the budget is due largely to increases in transfers and wage government consumption. Table 2.2 shows that governments regain control over the budget for more than a short period only when they cut exactly these two budget items.

Table 2.3 provides more direct evidence on this point. For each episode of expansion and consolidation, we calculate how much each budget item increased or decreased in the two years before the consolidation. We then compute by how much the government corrected the change in that budget item during the consolidation.

The first interesting result is that, on average, aggregate expenditure increased much more before unsuccessful consolidations than before the successful ones: 1.2% of GDP against 0.3%. Yet, as we have seen, successful consolidations cut expenditure much more than unsuccessful ones: 1.2% of GDP against 0.4%, so that at the end of successful consolidations expenditures are, on average, 0.8% of GDP lower than two years before

Table 2.3 Consolidation efforts and fiscal performance

	Success		Failure	
	Before	During	Before	During
Expenditures	0.3	−1.2	1.2	−0.4
	(0.7)	(−6.9)	(2.5)	(−2.0)
Investment	−0.3	−0.3	−0.1	−0.3
	(−1.7)	(−4.5)	(−1.4)	(4.4)
Transfers	0.6	−0.2	1.0	0.1
	(3.2)	(−3.5)	(3.6)	(0.9)
Consumption	0.1	−0.5	0.2	−0.1
	(0.5)	(−3.8)	(1.0)	(−1.4)
Wage expenditures	0.1	−0.3	0.0	0.0
	(0.5)	(−4.1)	(0.3)	(−0.4)
Non-wage consumption	0.0	−0.1	0.1	−0.1
	(0.4)	(−2.4)	(2.4)	(−3.1)
Subsidies	−0.2	−0.2	0.2	0.0
	(−1.3)	(−2.6)	(1.4)	(−0.7)
Revenues	0.7	1.2	1.0	1.9
	(1.9)	(6.5)	(2.7)	(9.3)
Taxes on income	0.6	0.5	0.8	1.1
	(2.4)	(3.1)	(2.4)	(5.2)
Taxes on business	0.0	0.3	0.0	0.3
	(0.2)	(2.9)	(0.0)	(3.2)
Indirect taxes	0.1	0.4	0.3	0.6
	(0.4)	(3.6)	(1.6)	(6.8)

Note: T-statistics in parentheses.

the consolidation, while at the end of unsuccessful consolidation expenditures are *higher* by 0.8% of GDP than two years before the consolidation! In percentage terms, successful consolidations correct about 350% on average of the increase in expenditures over the previous two years, while unsuccessful consolidations correct only about 35% – a difference by a factor of 10!

Successful consolidations correct ten times as much the preceding increase in expenditures over the previous years than unsuccessful consolidations.

Disaggregating expenditures, we see again the usual pattern of differences between the two types of consolidations. Successful consolidations correct drastically the accumulation of transfers and, especially, wage expenditures, while unsuccessful consolidations continue the increase in transfers and do virtually nothing to wage expenditures.

Thus, Table 2.3 summarizes clearly our main point: to regain sustainability of the budget, governments must *attack the problem at the source.*

3

Case studies

The following chapter presents case studies of fiscal stabilizations in a sample of European countries. Among these cases, the first Irish stabilization (1982–4) stands out as a clear example of failure. The Swedish case (1983–90) shows that the failure to control the driving force of spending in *good times* is a forerunner of debt explosion in *hard times*. In contrast, the second Irish stabilization (1987–9), the Danish stabilization episode (1983–6) and the British fiscal policy in the 1980s illustrate successful consolidation efforts. Finally, recent stabilization programmes in France (1994–6), Germany (1994–6) and Sweden (1994–6) and their prospects of success are considered. Unfortunately, the future fiscal performance of Germany and France looks rather bleak, while Sweden introduced some promising reforms.

3.1 | Failures in the 1980s

3.1.1   Ireland, 1982–4

Ireland embarked on a trajectory of growing debt in the early 1970s, fuelled by a massive rise in government expenditures.[10] At the turn of the decade, a weak economy and an unemployment rate rising from 7.1% in 1979 to 11.4% in 1982 worsened the already serious fiscal problems. The general government deficit mounted to more than 10% of GDP. Interest payments – at 6.6% of GDP in 1980/81 – put a serious strain on fiscal manoeuvrability. The debt burden rapidly increased from 62.5% of GDP in 1976/77 to 72.7% in 1980/81. The deficit problem continued to be based on the expenditure side and resulted particularly from primary spending increases in public investments and compensation of employees (see Table 3.1).

The coalition government coming to power in 1982[11] reacted to the fiscal deterioration with tax increases. During its first year in office, the government primarily raised social security contributions and indirect taxes. Later on, both indirect taxes and property taxes were adjusted upward (OECD Economic Survey – Ireland, 1985: 72, 75; de Haan *et al.*, 1992: 111). The government, however, pursued at best a mixed strategy to contain expenditures restraining government consumption[12] and capital expenditures, but at the same time opting for increased welfare payments, family income supplements and unemployment benefits (OECD Economic Survey – Ireland, 1985: 74, 76). Transfer payments increased by 3% of GDP compared to the pre-consolidation level. The net effect of these measures was an increase in government spending by 2.3 percentage points (see Table 3.1). Thus, the improvement of the primary balance during the time period was entirely based on revenues, while the deficit built-up had been caused by spending increases.

In fact, the consolidation effort started in 1982 completely failed to reduce debt and interest payments. Instead, the debt ratio rose from 72.7% of GDP in 1980/81 to 96.9% in 1983/84 and the share of interest payments in GDP increased from 6.6% of GDP to 8.9%. The fiscal performance worsened even further in the subsequent two years[13] (see Table 3.1).

Table 3.1   The first Irish stabilization

	76/77 (1)	80/81 (2)	83/84 (3)	85/86 (4)	Difference (2)–(1)	Difference (3)–(2)	Difference (4)–(3)
Debt	62.5	72.7	96.9	107.6	10.2	24.2	10.7
Balance	−7.7	−12.4	−10.2	−10.6	−4.7	2.2	−0.4
Revenues	35.4	36.2	40.6	40.3	0.8	4.4	−0.3
Expenditures	43.1	48.6	50.9	50.8	5.5	2.3	−0.1
Transfers	16.2	16.5	19.5	19.7	0.3	3.0	0.2
Wages	11.4	13.0	12.8	12.2	1.6	−0.2	−0.6
Purchases	5.1	5.8	5.0	5.0	0.7	−0.8	0.0
Investment	4.4	5.5	4.1	3.7	1.1	−1.4	−0.4
Interest payments	5.0	6.6	8.9	9.4	1.6	2.3	0.5
Primary balance	−2.7	−5.8	−1.4	−1.1	−3.1	4.4	0.3

Source: European Commission (1997b)

3.1.2   Sweden, 1983–90

The recession affecting the Swedish economy at the end of the 1970s spurred a fiscal deterioration that had started already in the middle of this decade. The debt ratio jumped from 28.2% of GDP in 1975/76 to 54.1% in 1981/82 and the budget balance fell from a surplus in the mid-1970s to −6.2% of GDP in 1981/82. The process of fiscal deterioration was the result of large spending growth. From 1975/76 to the early 1980s spending grew by 15.0% of GDP, most of which was accounted for by rising interest payments and transfers. Public wages also explain a quarter of the expenditure growth. During the same period, current revenues increased only 5.4% of GDP (see Table 3.2).

In October 1982, the Social Democratic government set forth a crisis programme. The government devalued the krona and planned to initiate a consolidation programme including higher taxes and a tight expenditure policy from 1983/84 onward (OECD Economic Survey – Sweden, 1985: 11). The Palme government complied with its goals of raising revenues by 2.5% of GDP[14] and reducing expenditures by 3.2% of GDP between 1982 and 1986. Wage expenditures and public investment were the prime targets of cuts. The share of public investment in GDP declined from 3.8% in 1982 to 2.6% in 1986 and public wage expenditures decreased by almost two percentage points during this period.[15] Transfers, however, remained stable due to a mixed policy, which included a 'compensatory' adjustment of the pension base rate for the devaluation effect and extended unemployment benefits, but downsized subsidies to industry, food and rents (OECD Economic Survey – Sweden, 1984: 52–3, 1985: 58).

Although the government was eventually able to stop debt growth in the mid-1980s, the debt ratio was 63.7% of GDP in 1985/86, up from 54.1% in 1981/82. The effort to control fiscal deficits and debt was successful from fiscal 1986/87 onward. The adjustment strategy of the Social Democratic successor government was again based on adjustments on both sides of the budget. Higher rates of indirect taxes and temporary measures yielded most of the revenue increases.[16] Most of the expenditure reductions, however, occurred in the initial period of the stabilization phase and were primarily targeted at capital expenditures.[17] In contrast, current spending increased after 1987 due to rising transfers and only moderate decreases in government consumption and investment spending in relation to GDP (see Table 3.2).

Table 3.2 The Swedish stabilization

	75/76 (1)	81/82 (2)	89/90 (3)	91/92 (4)	Difference (2)−(1)	Difference (3)−(2)	Difference (4)−(3)
Debt	28.2	54.1	44.5	60.1	25.9	−9.6	15.6
Balance	3.6	−6.2	4.8	−4.5	−9.8	11.0	−9.3
Revenues	53.8	59.2	65.1	61.3	5.4	5.9	−3.8
Expenditures	50.2	65.2	60.4	65.7	15.0	−4.8	5.3
Transfers	20.7	24.7	25.9	29.3	4.0	1.2	3.4
Wages	16.9	20.7	18.4	19.2	3.8	−2.3	0.8
Purchases	6.2	7.0	6.5	6.7	0.8	−0.5	0.2
Investment	4.1	6.1	2.5	2.5	2.0	−3.6	0.0
Interest payments	2.1	6.1	5.2	5.3	4.0	−0.9	0.1
Primary balance	5.8	−0.1	10.0	0.8	−5.9	10.1	−9.2

Source: European Commission (1997b)

At a first glance, the stabilization effort appears successful, since the debt ratio plummeted 9.6 percentage points during the consolidation phase and the fiscal balance showed an average surplus of 4.8% in 1989/90. However, the immediate aftermath of the stabilization phase, when the debt ratio exploded by almost 16 percentage points, reveals its low level of durability (see Table 3.2).

The Swedish government proved unable to resist spending pressures, so that transfer payments even increased during the period of stable growth in the second half of the decade. Thus, it does not seem surprising that transfers became by far the fastest growing spending category, when the country entered the economic recession at the turn of the decade accompanied by a deep fiscal crisis (see Section 3.3.3).

3.2 Successes in the 1980s

3.2.1 The United Kingdom, 1979–90

When the conservative government under Mrs Thatcher came to power in 1979, it inherited a fiscal balance that had shown persistent deficits from the first oil price shock onward. The main source of the imbalance was a strong increase in transfer payments and a falling share of revenues in GDP. The Thatcher government put major emphasis on deficit reduction as part of its general economic policy strategy. Moreover, the government announced its intention to reduce the expenditure ratio by 4%

of GDP during the first four years in office (von Hagen and Harden, 1994: 396). In the same year, however, the country plunged into a recession[18] putting strong cyclical pressure on the budget. Hence, the expenditure ratio rose 3.7% of GDP during these years, most of which resulted again from increased transfers.

Despite these developments, the Thatcher government was able to remain in control of the budget balance, even reduced the deficit, and lowered the debt level by 5.6% of GDP between 1977/78 and 1981/82 (see Table 3.3). This consolidation during the recession was based on tough expenditure cuts implying a decline of the cyclically adjusted expenditure share by 3.5 percentage points (OECD Economic Survey – United Kingdom, 1983: 25) and revenue-raising measures. Most notably, the government declared a 10% reduction of the number of public employees over the following four years[19] (Rajah and Smith, 1994: 93) and re-indexed pensions and social security benefits in 1980.[20] In addition, the public investment ratio was reduced by 45% from the late 1970s to the early 1980s (see Table 3.3). Revenues rose by 4.2% of GDP between 1977/78 and 1981/82, as the national insurance contributions were revised upward four times until 1983, a higher tax rate was imposed on North Sea oil production, and a supplementary tax was introduced in 1981.

These fiscal policies were accompanied by institutional changes to enforce expenditure constraint. A ministerial committee, the Star Chamber, was set up to strengthen the Treasury's position in the governmental budget negotiations. The base for budget planning changed from volume indicators to cash allowing for a better *ex ante* determination of spending. This replaced the cash limits, which had been imposed on different spending categories and local governments since the mid-1970s (see von Hagen and Harden, 1994). Finally, the Thatcher government dissolved the pay commission for public employees, which it held responsible for unduly large wage increases during its first years in office (Edwards *et al.*, 1995: 51).

After the recession years, the Thatcher government continued a disciplined fiscal policy, although the fiscal performance in terms of debt and deficit development worsened somewhat due to the costs of miners disputes in 1984–5 and rising interest payments (Edwards *et al.*, 1995: 57, OECD Economic Survey – United Kingdom, 1986: 15).[21] From 1985 onward, different spending measures were approved to achieve the government's goal of expenditure reduction.[22] More pressure was put on wages, so that real wages decreased by 1.6% from 1985 to 1990, the government

Table 3.3 UK fiscal policy in the 1980s

	78/79 (1)	81/82 (2)	89/90 (3)	91/92 (4)	Difference (2)–(1)	Difference (3)–(2)	Difference (4)–(3)
Debt	59.6	54.0	36.4	38.8	−5.6	−17.6	2.4
Balance	−3.9	−3.8	−0.8	−2.1	0.1	3.0	−1.3
Revenues	37.8	42.0	38.7	37.7	4.2	−3.3	−1.0
Expenditures	41.7	45.4	39.5	42.1	3.7	−5.9	2.6
Transfers	13.2	15.2	12.5	14.3	2.0	−2.7	1.8
Wages	12.4	13.0	11.5	12.0	0.6	−1.5	0.5
Purchases	7.5	8.5	8.0	9.2	1.0	−0.5	1.2
Investment	3.1	1.7	2.1	2.1	−1.4	0.4	0.0
Interest payments	4.3	5.0	3.6	3.0	0.7	−1.4	−0.6
Primary balance	0.4	1.6	2.8	−1.5	1.2	1.2	−4.3

Source: European Commission (1996a)

rescaled the state earnings-related pension scheme, industrial subsidies were curtailed drastically and social security, child and unemployment benefits were cut or restricted in several occasions (Pierson, 1996: 162–3; Rajah and Smith, 1994: 304). Moreover, a shrinking public enterprise sector and growing proceeds from privatization contributed as negative expenditures to the overall reduction (see GAO, 1994).

At the end of the 1980s, the government had in fact achieved a remarkable consolidation. The debt ratio fell from 54.0% of GDP in 1981/82 to 36.4% in 1989/90 and the deficit improved from an average of 3.9% of GDP in 1977/78 to 0.8% in 1989/90. The government maintained a primary surplus during the entire adjustment period from 1979 onward (European Commission, 1996a). Since tax policy primarily aimed at a lower tax burden on income and wealth from 1984 onward, the initial tax increase was strongly reverted and the adjustment was based on lower spending shares. Strong economic growth facilitated the expenditure measures during the second half of the decade, which led to a decline in government expenditures from 45.4% of GDP in 1981/82 to 39.5% in 1989/90. The biggest change occurred in transfer payments, which dropped from 15.2% of GDP in 1981/82 to 12.5% in 1989/90 falling below their pre-crisis level.

3.2.2 Ireland, 1987–9

After the failure of the previous consolidation attempt, the Irish government that took power in 1987 launched an adjustment programme that differed drastically from the previous episode (see Section 3.1.1). This time the programme tried to achieve consolidation primarily through spending measures. The expenditure ratio dropped 8.5% of GDP during the stabilization years, while revenues declined less than one percentage point (see Table 3.4). First, the government announced a package to reduce permanent public sector employees. The package included a hiring freeze, early retirement and voluntary redundancy schemes. The package was successfully implemented during the next years leading to a reduction in public sector employment by almost 10% until 1990 (de Haan *et al.*, 1992: 95).

Second, the government started a recovery programme sustained by a tri-partite agreement with the social partners. The programme established targets for limited public service growth and wage moderation in the public and private sector. The government made personal income tax concessions partly compensating for the wage policy, since the key measure of the tax reform taking effect in 1989 was a cut in the marginal tax rates on the income of households (Alesina and Perotti, 1997: 233, OECD Economic Survey – Ireland, 1988: 115–16). Additionally, capital and corporate taxes were reduced in 1990 (OECD Economic Survey – Ireland, 1991: 115), so that revenues diminished by 1.8% of GDP from 1985/86 to 1990/91 (see Table 3.4).

The restraint on wages and the reduction in public employment led to a decrease of wage expenditures by 1.5% of GDP during the following years. The most important break in expenditure policy, however, was the 1989 cut in transfers.[23]

Table 3.4 The second Irish stabilization

	85/86 (1)	88/89 (2)	90/91 (3)	Difference (2)–(1)	Difference (3)–(1)
Debt	107.6	105.2	95.1	−2.4	−10.1
Balance	−10.6	−3.1	−2.3	7.5	0.8
Revenues	40.3	39.3	37.5	−1.0	−1.8
Expenditures	50.8	42.3	39.8	−8.5	−2.5
Transfers	19.7	17.7	15.8	−2.0	−1.9
Wages	12.2	10.7	10.7	−1.5	0.0
Purchases	5.0	3.7	4.0	−1.3	0.4
Investment	3.7	1.8	2.2	−1.9	0.3
Interest payments	9.4	8.1	7.6	−1.3	−0.5
Primary balance	−1.1	5.0	5.3	6.1	0.3

Source: European Commission (1997b)

Transfers to enterprises were nominally reduced by 27% and stood well under their previous level for the following period. Even transfers to households were reduced by 1.6% of GDP in nominal terms.[24] Overall, the expenditure restraint curtailed spending from 50.8% of GDP in 1985/86 to 42.3% in 1989/90. The primary balance improved remarkably and turned positive in 1987. The improvement in the structural balance[25] and the lasting success of the consolidation phase prove that this success cannot be solely attributed to the general economic upswing during the second half of the 1980s. A visible effect of the stabilization strategy was a reduction of the debt ratio by 10.1% of GDP until 1990/91 (see Table 3.4).[26]

3.2.3   Denmark, 1983–6

The Danish economy deteriorated rapidly at the beginning 1980s. Macroeconomic conditions accelerated the growth of debt which had already started in the mid-1970s. When a new coalition government came to power, the deficit had deteriorated from 0.4% in 1978 to 9.1% in 1982, and the debt level had jumped from 31.0% to 63.9% during the same period (European Commission, 1996a).

The government announced a major fiscal adjustment programme for the following four years. The programme worked equally through revenue increases and expenditure restraints. Expenditures were reduced from 59.3% of GDP in 1981/82 to 56.2% in 1985/86 and revenues increased from 51.3% of GDP to 56.9% (see Table 3.5). In the pre-adjustment period, compensation of employees and transfers were the two fastest growing expenditure categories. The fiscal programme of 1982 aimed at a reduction of these two categories.

In 1982, price indexation of certain transfer programmes was abolished, the maximum rate of daily cash benefits was frozen and sickness coverage was reduced. Public employee pensions were particularly affected by these restraints. From 1983 to 1985 transfers to local authorities were cut further (Alesina and Perotti, 1997: 237). Due to these measures and the resurgent economy, transfers could be reduced from 22% of GDP in 1982 to 19.3% in 1986. Moreover, the semi-automatic regulation of public sector wages, i.e. the indexation and the automatic link to wage increases in the private sector, was suspended until 1987, while wages were virtually frozen (OECD Economic Survey – Denmark, 1983: 50). The result of these measures was a strong

Table 3.5   The Danish stabilization

	81/82 (1)	85/86 (2)	87/88 (3)	Difference (2)–(1)	Difference (3)–(2)
Debt	57.5	67.9	60.5	10.4	−7.4
Balance	−8.0	0.7	1.5	8.7	0.8
Revenues	51.3	56.9	58.4	5.6	1.5
Expenditures	59.3	56.2	56.9	−3.1	0.7
Transfers	21.7	19.7	20.9	−2.0	1.2
Wages	19.9	17.6	18.3	−2.3	0.7
Purchases	7.3	6.2	6.3	−1.1	0.1
Investment	2.9	1.9	1.9	−1.0	−0.1
Interest payments	5.7	9.4	8.2	3.7	−1.2
Primary balance	−2.4	10.0	9.7	12.4	−0.3

Source: European Commission (1996a)

reduction in the government wage bill, amounting to more than the combined reduction in government purchases and capital spending. On the revenue side, direct taxes and social security contributions increased the most (OECD Economic Survey – Denmark, 1984: 50–1, 1986: 12).

As a consequence of these measures, the budget balance improved rapidly from a deficit level of 8% of GDP in 1981/82 to a surplus of 0.7% in 1985/86. Debt continued to grow during the initial years of the crisis, but reached a turning point in 1984. During the second half of the stabilization phase a declining trend began which was sustained beyond the adjustment (see Table 3.5).

3.3   Three recent adjustments – prospects of success?

3.3.1   France, 1994–6

France showed signs of economic recovery in 1994, when the government announced a programme of fiscal restraint to stabilize the budget balance. During the previous years of economic recession, government non-interest expenditures had grown steadily from 47.2% of GDP in 1989 to 51.0% in 1994, while revenues remained fairly constant at around 49% of GDP. Correspondingly, the balance deteriorated from −1.2% of GDP in 1989 to −5.6% in 1994 and the debt ratio increased by 14.0

Table 3.6 France in the 1990s

	1989 (1)	1994 (2)	1996 (3)	Difference (2)−(1)	Difference (3)−(2)
Debt	34.4	48.4	56.2	14.0	7.8
Balance	−1.2	−5.6	−4.1	−4.4	1.5
Revenues	48.7	49.0	50.4	0.3	1.4
Expenditures	49.9	54.6	54.5	4.7	−0.1
Transfers	25.5	28.1	28.4	2.6	0.3
Consumption	18.0	19.4	19.3	1.4	−0.1
Wages	13.3	14.2	14.4	0.9	0.2
Purchases	2.9	3.2	4.9	0.3	1.7
Investment	3.4	3.2	3.0	−0.2	−0.2
Interest payments	2.7	3.6	3.8	0.9	0.2
Primary balance	1.5	−2.0	−0.3	−3.5	1.7

Source: European Commission (1997b)

percentage points (see Table 3.6). Most of the expenditure expansion can be attributed to transfers, which increased by almost 3% of GDP between 1989 and 1994, more than any other spending category.

In line with the convergence programme for EMU and the five-year budget law, the stabilization effort initiated in 1994 was aimed primarily at expenditure restraint.[27] Expenditures were to be kept stable in real terms and the deficit had to be reduced. In the end, however, revenue increases and expenditure reductions contributed almost equally to the adjustment. On the revenue side, indirect taxes were set at higher levels in 1995 and the government could incorporate some privatization proceeds. The effect of the pension reform introduced in 1993 and of measures taken in 1994 to reduce the growth of health care expenditures vanished, as the government took several expansionary spending initiatives in favour of employment, the housing sector and small and medium-sized enterprises and pensioners in 1995. When additional pressure on the budget emerged from higher interest rates, the government reacted with a restriction on wage increases and transfers to local government in 1996. These initiatives led to a relative downward adjustment in government consumption and transfers. The source of the problem, however, was not effectively addressed, since transfers contributed about one-half to the rising primary deficits until 1994 and increased again in 1996 (see Table 3.6). The primary deficit improved from 2.0% of GDP to 0.3% during the adjustment phase and the total deficit fell moderately from 5.6% of GDP in 1994 to 4.1% in

1996, remaining well above the 3% threshold of the Maastricht Treaty. Finally, the debt ratio continued to grow, albeit at a decelerating pace reaching 56.2% of GDP in 1996 (see Table 3.6).

3.3.2 Germany, 1994–6

Germany's fiscal performance during the early 1990s was driven by two factors: unification and recession. The impact of unification amounted to massive transfers between 4% and 5% of GDP (OECD Economic Survey – Germany, 1994: 54). The adjustment problems in East Germany proved more severe than expected and the situation worsened when the West German economy entered a recession.

A fiscal retrenchment programme was adopted in 1993 as part of an overall social pact to end the unification period. The federal government assumed the debt of the former GDR and various semi-governmental institutions in the context of the unification in 1995. The government also took over the debt of the German railways. These stock effects explain a large part of the increase in public debt from 48.2% of GDP in 1993 to 60.7% in 1996. The fiscal programme was complemented by additional measures to achieve a medium-term fiscal consolidation.[28]

The retrenchment programme included cuts in unemployment and related transfers, an increase in mineral oil tax and several measures to reduce tax expenditures. Moreover, the pension contribution rate was raised. At the same time, however,

Table 3.7 Germany in the 1990s

	1992 (1)	1993 (2)	1994 (3)	1996 (4)	Difference (2)–(1)	Difference (4)–(2)
Debt	44.1	48.2	50.4	60.7	4.1	12.5
Balance	−2.8	−3.5	−2.4	−3.8	−0.7	−0.3
Revenues	46.0	46.4	46.8	45.6	0.4	−0.8
Expenditures	48.9	49.9	49.3	49.3	1.0	−0.6
Transfers	21.2	22.4	22.6	22.9	1.2	0.5
Consumption	20.0	20.1	19.6	19.6	0.1	−0.5
Wages	10.6	10.8	10.4	10.2	0.2	−0.6
Purchases	8.7	8.5	8.4	8.7	−0.2	0.2
Investment	2.8	2.8	2.7	2.3	0.0	−0.5
Interest payments	3.3	3.3	3.4	3.7	0.0	0.4
Primary balance	0.4	−0.2	1.0	−0.1	−0.6	0.1

Source: European Commission (1997b)

taxes on corporations and business profits were reduced as part of a general tax reform (OECD Economic Survey – Germany, 1993: 89–90, 1994: 59). Renewed consolidation efforts emerged in 1995/96, when the government increased taxes on insurance and wealth, the 'solidarity' income-tax surcharge was extended and contributions to a new insurance system alleviated the heavy deficits incurred in pension and health insurance funds (OECD Economic Survey – Germany, 1995: 62). On the expenditure side, a reduction in social assistance payments and a phased reform of pension benefits prolonging working age was approved. Additionally, the finance minister enacted expenditure controls in 1996.

In spite of these efforts, primary spending was reduced only modestly from 46.6% of GDP to 45.6%, as transfers remained the main source of spending pressure and increased from 22.4% of GDP to 22.9% between 1993 and 1996. In addition, the revenue share fell by 0.8% of GDP during these years. As a consequence, the government balance started to deteriorate again after a short-lived improvement in 1994 and the debt ratio continued to rise. In 1996, the total deficit reached 3.8% of GDP and the debt ratio exceeded the 60% of GDP limit set in the Maastricht Treaty (see Table 3.7).

3.3.3 Sweden, 1994–6

The deterioration of Sweden's economic and fiscal position in the early 1990s was unprecedented in the country's recent history. The economic recession was partly a correction of the overheating of the economy in the late 1980s due to financial deregulation, asset price boom and insufficient fiscal restraint.[29] Unemployment climbed from 1.6% to 8.2% in 1992, which proved devastating for public finances due to the high elasticity of the budget to cyclical unemployment. Revenues decreased from 65.3% of GDP in 1989 to 60.3% in 1993 due to a tax reform, which the Social Democratic government implemented early in 1991, and the termination of several temporary taxes (OECD Economic Survey – Sweden, 1994: 28). Primary expenditures, on the other hand, rapidly increased from 54.6% to 66.4% between 1989 and 1993. By far the fastest growing spending category were transfers, which climbed by 7% of GDP.[30] This drove the primary balance from 10.8% to 6.1% between 1989 and 1993, while the debt ratio rose from 45.5% of GDP in 1989 to 76.0% in 1994 (see Table 3.8).

Table 3.8   Sweden in the 1990s

	1989 (1)	1993 (2)	1996 (3)	Difference (2)–(1)	Difference (3)–(2)
Debt	45.5	76.0	77.7	30.5	1.7
Balance	5.4	−12.3	−3.6	−17.7	8.7
Revenues	65.3	60.3	62.6	−5.0	2.3
Direct taxes	25.2	20.8	22.2	−4.4	1.4
Indirect taxes	16.2	15.6	15.9	−0.6	0.3
Social security	15.2	14.4	15.3	−0.8	0.9
Expenditures	60.0	72.6	66.2	12.6	−6.4
Transfers	25.7	33.1	30.7	7.4	−2.4
Consumption	26.2	28.1	25.9	1.9	−2.2
Wages	17.9	19.2	17.8	1.3	−1.4
Purchases	6.3	7.1	8.1	0.8	1.0
Investment	2.5	1.1	2.6	−1.4	1.5
Interest payments	5.4	6.2	7.1	0.8	0.9
Primary balance	10.8	−6.1	3.5	−16.9	9.6

Source: European Commission (1997b)

The economy started to recover, when a new Social Democratic government came into power in 1994 and declared a fiscal consolidation programme. The first part of the package was introduced in November and the government put forward additional budget bills in January and April of the following year. The revenue measures increased taxes on property, income and corporate gains. More importantly, transfers to households were reduced in almost all spending categories. The indexation of social transfers was limited, child allowances were decreased and pensions reduced. In 1996, replacement rates in social security schemes were reduced by five percentage points and social security contributions raised. In the same year, a budget bill implementing a system of expenditure ceilings for 1997 to 1999 was approved as part of a general reform of the budget process (see Box 4.1, p. 38) setting reduced deficit targets for the following years. A consequence of this belt-tightening was a decline of primary expenditures by 7.3% of GDP between 1993 and 1996. Most of the reduction resulted from a reduction of transfers by 2.4% of GDP. Similarly, government wage expenditures grew less than GDP, while investments and purchases increased their budget share (see Table 3.8). In addition, revenues contributed almost the same amount to the fiscal recovery they had contributed to the deterioration. In particular, the drastic effect of the previous tax reform on direct taxes was partly reversed. The primary balance improved dramatically from −6.1% of GDP in 1993 to 3.5% in 1996 and the government could stop the debt explosion. In fact, the debt ratio fell from 79% of GDP to 77.7% from 1994 to 1996 (European Commission, 1997b).

3.3.4 One up, two down: Sweden, France and Germany

What are the prospects for a successful fiscal adjustment in these three countries? The initial deficit improvement in Germany was quickly reverted, debt continued to grow and the problem of rising transfers was not effectively addressed. France continued to reduce its deficit, but not enough to stabilize its debt, and the expenditure reduction was too moderate given its contribution to the prior fiscal deterioration. We conclude that this is bad news for the prospect of lasting fiscal consolidations in these two countries.

In contrast, Sweden has forcefully corrected transfers, the main spending source of the growing deficit, and significantly increased taxes. Furthermore, it has reformed the institutional setting and succeeded to improve deficits and lower its debt level. Hence, this country has made real progress toward restoring control over its public finances.

4

Budgeting institutions and sustainability

Non-sustainability of public finances ultimately reflects weaknesses and flaws in a country's fiscal institutions.

In Chapter 1, we have argued that a reliable assessment of a country's public finances must distinguish between the symptoms and the sources of a loss of sustainability. To remedy the sources and regain lasting control over spending and deficits, institutional changes are required. Chapters 2 and 3 have focused on the symptoms. In this chapter, we turn to the sources.

Our main contention here is that non-sustainability of public finances ultimately reflects weaknesses and flaws in a country's fiscal institutions, i.e. the institutional framework governing the decision-making processes over government spending, revenues and deficits. These institutions comprise the formal and informal decision-making rules that distribute authority over public finances, determine who does what and when in the decision-making process, and channel the flow of information among the relevant actors.

A good starting point for the analysis of budgeting institutions is to realize the fact that all decisions on spending, taxation and borrowing have implications for the distribution of the benefits and costs of government activities. The distributional perspective suggests two channels whereby weaknesses in the decision-making processes lead to excessive spending and deficits:

- Policy-makers do not completely internalize the social costs of spending and opt for excessive spending and deficits.

- Policy-makers refrain from imposing adjustment costs on their constituency or disagree about the distribution of the costs, when consolidation is needed.

4.1 | Fragmentation of the budget process

The problem of incomplete internalization of the costs of government activities arises when public revenues are largely generated by general taxes on individuals, business and corporations, while the programmes that the money is spent on target specific social groups and political constituencies. In such situations, common to all modern democracies, policy-makers are willing to engage in excessive spending, because the individual constituencies benefiting from public policy programmes do not bear their full costs, but devolve part of them to others.

Building on a tradition in American political science,[31] one can interpret this feature of the government budget process as a common-pool resource problem. In the American form of the argument, politicians representing individual electoral districts are viewed as using the budget process to channel money taken out of a general tax fund into public policy projects benefiting their districts. The incongruence between the spatial incidence of the costs and benefits of these projects creates a tendency to overestimate the net marginal benefit from spending. As a result, government spending grows too large, and so does the general tax burden. Much like a common pool excessively exploited by private fishermen, the general tax fund is overexploited by the representatives of individual spending interests. Applying this paradigm to a European political context, where politicians often represent country-wide groups in society rather than regions or electoral districts, requires a translation of the geographical dimension into one of different constituencies in society. Still, politicians representing different groups in society spend money taken out of a general tax fund on programmes aimed at different groups in society.[32] As long as the recipient groups can be defined clearly, this translation is possible, and the incongruence between the beneficiaries of individual programmes and the general taxpayer remains.

Putting the argument into a dynamic context, one can show that the common-pool problem results in excessive deficits and debts, and a tendency to delay reaction to exogenous shocks to spending and revenues.[33]

The core of the argument then is that public budgeting involves an externality – money used to finance narrowly targeted projects being taken out of a general tax fund – and a coordination failure among the relevant decision-makers. In the example of a fishery, this failure is the more severe, the larger

Public budgeting involves an externality and a coordination failure among the relevant policy-makers.

the number of fishermen exploiting the common pool. The analogy suggests that the tendency to spend more, to run large deficits, and to postpone reaction to exogenous shocks increases with the number of representatives of individual spending interests that are allowed to make autonomous spending decisions, i.e. the more *fragmented* the budget process is. Since the most important representatives of individual spending interests in European governments are the individual spending ministers, the most straightforward implication of this proposition is that government spending and deficits are the larger, the larger is the number of spending departments and ministers in a country's government. Kontopoulos and Perotti (1997), using data from OECD countries, show that this proposition is indeed confirmed empirically.

Interpreting the problem of excessive spending and deficits as a coordination failure leads one to look at other common-pool problems in practice for solutions. Political economy emphasizes the importance of decision-making rules that promote a comprehensive view of the common-pool resource, i.e. one that takes the full benefits and costs of an increased use of the resource into consideration. The opposing power to fragmentation is thus *centralization* of the budget process, the existence of institutions forcing the representatives of individual groups in society to recognize the true marginal cost and benefit of the projects financed from the general tax fund, and thus to internalize the budgeting externality.

There are two basic institutional approaches to achieve centralization: delegation and contracts.

In the context of government budgeting, there are two basic institutional approaches to achieve centralization: *delegation* and *contracts*. Both can be found among the budget processes in Europe (von Hagen, 1992). Under a delegation approach, the participants in the budget process agree to delegate significant decision-making powers to an agent who makes some important decisions for them, usually the finance minister, since the latter is not bound by special interests to the same extent as a minister heading a spending department, instead, his constituency is the general taxpayer. Internalizing the relevant externalities, the agent will then make more efficient decisions.

The delegation approach builds on the following key characteristics:

- A finance minister vested with strong agenda-setting power relative to the remaining members of the executive; typically, this involves the right to make binding proposals for the broad budgetary categories and information advantages.

- A finance minister vested with strong monitoring capacity in the implementation of the budget and the power to correct deviations from the budget plan, e.g. through cash limits and the requirement of disbursement approvals from the finance department.

- A strong position of the executive relative to the legislature in the parliamentary phase of the budget process; this involves strict limitations on the scope of parliamentary amendments to the executive's budget proposal and a limited role of the upper house of parliament in the process where applicable.

France is probably the best example for delegation to a fiscal agent in the European Union (von Hagen and Harden, 1994). The annual budget process starts with a directive issued by the finance minister and the prime minister fixing the financial ceilings for all spending ministries for the next budget. These ceilings are strictly observed in the rest of the process. Parliament operates under amendment restrictions ruling out any increase in spending or decrease in taxes without proposing an offsetting change on the same side of the budget. The executive can pass entire sections of the budget law in an accelerated procedure with practically no parliamentary debate. During the year, the finance minister controls the execution strictly. Britain and Germany are the other examples of countries relying on delegation.

Under a contract approach, the participants start the budget process by negotiating and agreeing on a set of key budgetary parameters, usually spending targets for the individual spending departments. Here, it is the process of negotiation that makes the participants realize the externalities created by the general tax fund.[34] The contract approach is characterized by the following features of the process:

- A strong emphasis on budgetary targets negotiated among all members of the executive at the beginning of the annual budget cycle and which are regarded as binding for all spending departments; often these targets are backed up by a multiannual fiscal programme as part of the coalition contract among the ruling parties.

- A finance minister vested with strong monitoring capacities in the implementation of the budget, yet little agenda setting powers.

■ A weak position of the executive relative to the parliament exemplified by weak or no limits on parliamentary amendments to the budget proposal.

A good example of the contract approach in Europe is the Danish budget process after 1982 (von Hagen and Harden, 1994). The process started annually with a round of negotiations among all partners of the coalition government fixing the financial ceilings of all spending agencies. Running over these ceilings would have shaken the coalition. During these negotiations, however, the finance minister played no special role.

To evaluate the importance of centralization of the budget process for budget deficits and debts, von Hagen and Harden (1994, 1996) following von Hagen (1992) construct an *index of centralization* capturing the most important features of the budget process in European governments. A high value on the index, which ranges from zero to 16, indicates the prevalence of strong elements of centralization in a country's budget process.

Figure 4.1 Budget processes, deficits and debt

Note: OECD Economic Outlook (1997), European Commission (1996a) and von Hagen and Harden (1995). Deficit and debt averages are based on the period 1981–95.

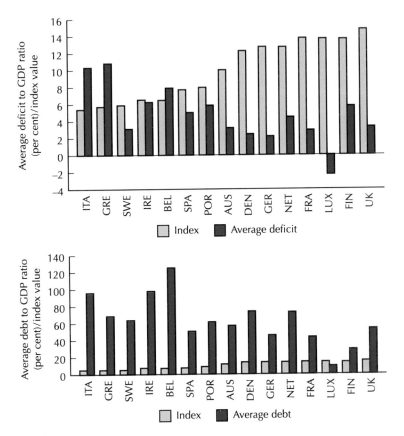

Figure 4.1 shows this index together with the average deficit ratios and debt ratios of the EU countries over the 1980s and 1990s. The upper chart clearly shows that countries with a low degree of centralization have larger deficits than countries with a high degree of centralization. This confirms the main contention of the *common-pool* interpretation of the budget process. The lower chart shows that the same conclusion can be reached regarding the level of public debt. Strengthening institutions that reduce fragmentation of budget decisions and promote a comprehensive view of the costs and benefits of government activities reduces the government deficit.

Statistical tests confirm this visual impression. The rank correlation between the degree of centralization of a country's budget process as measured by the index and its average deficit over the period considered is significant and negative ($\rho = -0.69$). Similarly, the rank correlation between the degree of centralization of the budget process and the debt ratio is significant and negative ($\rho = -0.60$). Both rank correlations indicate that countries whose budget processes contain relatively strong elements of centralization managed to keep their deficits and debts relatively low over the recent past.

While these figures provide a more long-run perspective of the problem, Table 4.1 reports the results of a regression of annual change in government debt on the index of centralization and a

Reducing the fragmentation of budget decisions leads to lower deficits and debt.

Table 4.1   Determinants of government deficits

Variable	Coefficient	t-value
Constant	3.6	4.1
Lagged dependent variable	0.3	5.9
Real GDP growth rate	-0.9	-5.7
Change in unemployment rate	0.8	2.7
Real interest rate	-0.1	-0.7
Coalition of 2–3 parties	0.9	1.3
Coalition of 4–5 parties	0.8	0.4
Minority government	-0.2	-0.3
Change in government composition	1.6	3.6
Left-wing government	-0.5	-0.8
Index of centralization	-0.1	-2.1

Note: Sample 1981–94, all EU countries, 199 degrees of freedom. $R^2 = 0.51$. The dependent variable is the annual change in the debt ratio. The variables called 'coalition of *n* parties', 'change in government composition', and 'minority government' are dummy variables whose values are one under the specified circumstances for the year.

BOX 4.1   Institutions and fiscal performance – empirical evidence

Fragmentation leads to higher deficits and spending growth

Kontopoulos and Perotti (1997) measure fragmentation by the number of policy-makers involved in the budget process. Their study reveals that, in the 1970s, large cabinets exercised less effective control over the growth of expenditures and deficits than small cabinets. Insufficient spending control was particularly strong for transfers and the remuneration of government employees. During the 1980s and 1990s, when there was more room for ideologically motivated fiscal policies, smaller cabinets were more effective in consolidating and reversing the fiscal excesses of the 1970s.

Centralization reduces deficits and debt

Von Hagen (1992) and von Hagen and Harden (1994, 1996) show that the degree of centralization of the budget process, as measured by their empirical index, leads to more fiscal discipline, i.e. lower deficits and debt, in the sample of EU countries during the 1970s and 1980s. Hallerberg and von Hagen (1997a) show that budget processes based on delegation or contracts mitigate the deficit bias created by political instability. Hallerberg and von Hagen (1997b) show that the same institutional mechanisms reduce the effect of 'electoral business cycles' on the government deficit.

Alesina *et al.* (1995) find that hierarchically structured budget processes induced lower primary deficits among the Latin American countries in the 1980s and 1990s. Stein *et al.* (1997), working with data on OECD and Latin American countries, confirm this finding and, in addition, conclude that the disciplining effect extends to the debt level and total deficits.

Strauch (1997) uses an institutional index to assess the degree of centralization inherent in the budget processes of the US states. Analysing state budgets in the 1980s and 1990s, he finds that centralization led to lower expenditures and smaller deficits. This result holds as much for total budgets as for primary spending and deficits.

Strength of the fiscal bureaucracy reduces deficits

Hahm *et al.* (1994) analyse the strength of the fiscal bureaucracy in nine parliamentary democracies and find that strong fiscal bureaucracies are able to achieve lower deficits. Strength of the bureaucracy, here, measures the centralization of fiscal planning within the ministry of finance, the independence of the ministerial senior officials and the dominance of the finance minister vis-à-vis the spending ministers. Thus, their study indicates that a strong financed minister backed by a politically independent and centralized staff is conducive to fiscal discipline.

number of control variables. Here again, the index has a significant and negative coefficient, indicating that a larger degree of centralization comes with a lower level of deficits.

In addition, Hallerberg and von Hagen (1997b) and von Hagen and Harden (1994) show that countries ranking high on the index of centralization conducted more effective counter-cyclical stabilization policies. Thus, the fear that less deficit-prone budget processes become overly rigid and prevent effective stabilization is not empirically warranted. However, Hallerberg and von Hagen show that countries ranking high on the index of centralization are less likely to run large deficits in election years; this points to the greater dynamic efficiency of their fiscal policies. More empirical evidence on the impact of budget institutions on fiscal performance is reported in Box 4.1.

4.2 | Institutional reform and institutional choice

The potential of institutions to improve sustainability becomes apparent, when states pursuing successful adjustment programmes engage in institutional reform to make their consolidation efforts last. Several examples can be found in Europe in last two decades.

The potential of institutions to improve sustainability becomes apparent, when states pursuing successful adjustments engage in institutional reform.

In the early 1980s, the UK government introduced the 'Star Chamber' to contain the ministerial spending bias. The Star Chamber, a ministerial committee, was used between 1982 and 1988 to reconcile conflicts between the Treasury and individual spending ministers. The important aspect of the Star Chamber during the years of operation was that it was staffed by senior non-spending ministers to support the Treasury in bargaining with spending ministers. Since the UK budget process relies less on written guidelines, but heavily on the Treasurer's strategic position, this was an important ingredient for budgetary stringency (von Hagen and Harden, 1994).

While the United Kingdom provides an example for increasing centralization under a delegation approach, Denmark in the early 1980s provides an example for doing the same under a contract approach. As mentioned above, the Danish government adopted a budget process based on binding spending targets negotiated at the outset of the annual budget cycle. These targets were backed up by a longer-run strategy to reduce spending and increase productivity at the level of the individual spending departments.

BOX 4.2   Budget processes in Sweden and Ireland – institutional changes

Ireland and Sweden have changed their budget processes as part of the fiscal consolidation process. In Sweden the institutional changes were explicitly designed to cope with the fiscal crisis of the early 1990s. Sweden has improved the structure of governmental and parliamentary decision-making as much as budget transparency. In the reformed process, budget decisions are strongly constraint by multiannual nominal expenditure ceilings and the minister of finance sets the agenda for the governmental budget negotiations. Now, any amendments to the executive budget in the parliament have to be off-setting. The transparency of the budget greatly increased, since all special funds are included, the budget is submitted in one document and government loans to non-government entities are included in the budget. Finally, cash limits are tested in different areas during the implementation phase and carry over possibilities require the consent of the minister of finance.

In Ireland, fiscal targets became part of the pact with the social partners from 1987 onwards. Since 1992 commitment to the Maastricht criteria was explicitly included in the coalition agreements (von Hagen 1997: 11). To implement these targets, the Irish governments have changed their budget practice. First of all, they strengthened above all the position of the minister of finance within the government negotiations and during the budget implementation. Now the minister negotiates bilaterally with the spending ministers, has to approve disbursements and has the power to block expenditures. Since the parliament cannot amend the governmental proposal, this endows the minister of finance with strong agenda-setting throughout the entire decision-making process. The graph below, using the numerical measure developed by von Hagen (1992), illustrates the degree of centralization inherent in the budget process during the preparation, approval and implementation stages as well as the transparency of the budget before and after the recent reforms.

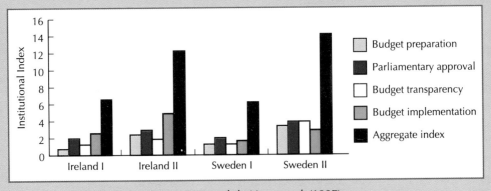

Source: von Hagen (1992) and de Haan *et al.* (1997)

Sweeping changes in the budget process also occurred in Ireland and Sweden in the late 1980s and 1990s; see Box 4.2. Both countries followed the contract approach. As indicated in Chapter 3, both countries were able to achieve a lasting fiscal consolidation on this basis.

In the 1990s, the Excessive Deficit Procedure together with the Convergence Programmes demanded by the Maastricht Treaty in preparation of EMU is another, important example of institutional reform of the budget process. The emphasis on multiannual targets and the regular review procedure required by the Treaty make the Convergence Procedure resemble a budget process under the contract approach. The main difference with a conventional contract-based budget process such as the Danish one is that the Convergence Procedure relies on the European Council and the Commission to enforce the fiscal targets. Thus, enforcement is the role of an agent external to domestic politics. Before the start of EMU, the ultimate penalty for violating the fiscal targets is the denial of membership in the EMU. For the EMU member states, the Excessive Deficit Procedure as strengthened by the Stability and Growth Pact of the Treaty of Amsterdam will continue this *external-enforcement* version of the contract approach, with financial fines as the ultimate penalty for violating the targets.

A proper working of these procedures would, of course, have implied a gradual reduction of the debt ratios of the EU countries. In fact, the opposite happened: the EU's average debt ratio was 60% in 1992, it climbed to 73% in 1996. Importantly, this increase was entirely driven by the debt expansions in five states: Germany (44% to 61%), France (40% to 56%), Spain (48% to 70%), Italy (109% to 124%), and the UK (42% to 55%). In contrast, the debt ratios of the other states were stabilized or fell after 1992.[35] The institutional change introduced with the Convergence Programmes and the Excessive Deficit Procedure worked very effectively for some states, but failed for others.

This mixed experience with the Excessive Deficit Procedure and the Convergence Programmes teaches an important lesson: one institutional model (the external-enforcement based contract approach) is not fit for solving the problem of non-sustainable public finances in all countries. The general argument is that two institutional approaches to solving the common-pool problem of public budgeting are suited for different types of governments (Hallerberg and von Hagen, 1997a). Delegation is the proper approach for single-party governments, while contracting is

Delegation is the proper approach for single-party governments, while contracting is better suited for multi-party governments.

better suited for multiparty governments. In a nutshell, it is difficult for a coalition government to work under a strong finance minister, since the latter necessarily comes from one of the coalition parties. Vesting him with special authorities would raise concerns among the other parties about a fair treatment of their spending interests in the budget process. At the same time, a commitment to fiscal targets is harder to keep for a single-party government, since there is no effective threat against reneging on the targets.[36]

Two factors matter critically in the current context. The first is the national electoral system. Since electoral systems of proportional representation are most likely to produce coalition governments, the contract approach is the more adequate one for states with such systems. In contrast, plurality electoral systems typically produce one-party governments, which makes the delegation approach more adequate for states with such systems. Among the EU states, the suggested pattern of institutional choice is strongly confirmed. As shown in Table 4.2, states with proportional representation (PR) systems chose a contract approach to the budget process, if they chose an institutional solution to the common-pool problem at all. In contrast, states with plurality systems chose a delegation approach as a solution.[37]

Table 4.2 Electoral systems and institutional choice

Electoral system	Institutional choice		
	Contract	Delegation	None
Proportional representation (PR)			
A, B, DK, SF, IRL, L, NL, P, E, S	A, B, DK, SF, IRL, L, NL, P		I, E, S*
Countries with PR and restrictive minimum vote requirement			
D		D	
Countries with plurality systems			
F, GRE, UK		F, UK	GRE

Source: von Hagen (1997)
Note: * Sweden has recently moved toward a targeting approach (see Box 4.2).
Key to countries: A (Austria), B (Belgium), D (Germany), DK (Denmark), E (Spain), F (France), GRE (Greece), I (Italy), IRL (Ireland), L (Luxembourg), NL (Netherlands), P (Portugal), S (Sweden), SF (Finland), UK (United Kingdom).

Furthermore, an institutional process relying on external enforcement presupposes that the external political agent enforcing the fiscal targets carries a large weight in the internal political process. A country's size is probably a first indicator of the importance of an external enforcement body: small countries pay more attention to international organizations than large countries, and the more so, the more they receive transfers from the same external organization.

Clearly, both arguments come to play in the experience with the Excessive Deficit Procedure and the Convergence Programmes. France, Britain and Germany fit into the explanation on two accounts. Their electoral systems make them more likely to adopt a delegation approach than a contracting approach. Fiscal targets such as those demanded by the Maastricht Treaty are difficult to sustain in the domestic political environment of these countries. All three are also large, so that threats by the European Commission and the European Council do not weigh as heavily in internal politics as in small countries. Italy and Spain would seem more fit for the target-oriented approach of the Maastricht Treaty on the basis of their electoral systems, but here the size argument counts strongly again.

Obviously, if the same institutional model does not fit all countries, institutional choice is a difficult and important matter, in which a country's political, economic and cultural characteristics all come to play. The implication, however, is not to put aside the importance of institutional reforms as an element of regaining sustainability of public finances. Instead, it is important to recognize that institutional reform must take into account the peculiarities of the national political systems. Attacking the problem at the source, in this context, means that institutional reform should be based on national solutions.

Attacking the problem at the source, in this context, means that institutional reform should be based on national solutions.

4.3 The budget process and other institutions

Another important source of losing control over spending and deficits is the spread of non-decisions in the budget process. Non-decisions occur when government expenditures are left to be determined by developments exogenous to the budget process rather than by discretionary decisions within its realm. Prime examples are the indexation of spending programmes to the price level or aggregate nominal income (government wage

BOX 4.3 Public sector wages and wage-setting institutions

European states have different modes of wages setting in the public sector. Several states devolve the determination of wages and public employment to collective bargaining at the regional and local levels or use wage indexation to correct for inflation and private sector developments. The figure below provides suggestive evidence that the growth of wage payments in the general government area, in fact, is related to the say the central government has in wage determination and the involvement of the finance minister or another non-spending minister. A high index indicates that the finance minister participates in wage negotiations, there is only a central level of bargaining, collective agreements with unions have to be approved by the parliament or another central entity and no indexation occurs. Notably, the successful Irish adjustment rests on tight wage-setting institutions. In comparison, the problems of the Spanish government to contain spending can be explained by its relatively weak influence on wage payments at lower levels of government.

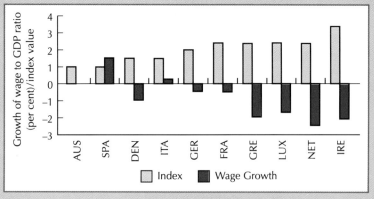

Note: European Commission (1996a) and PUMA (1994). Growth is the difference between the average wage to GDP ratio for 1981–5 and 1991–5. The Spearman rank correlation is −0.82 (p = 0.007).

bills or social security payments), and welfare expenditures based on entitlements the parameters of which are fixed by law or decree. Note that there is nothing 'natural' about determining wage, social security and welfare expenditures outside the annual budget process. Indeed, setting the relevant parameters is a part of the annual budget process in some countries (von Hagen and Harden, 1994; see Box 4.3 on wage setting). As a political strategy of *blame avoidance*,[38] however, non-decisions allow policy-makers to forego decisions that would seem tough on their constituencies. While being convenient for the policy-maker, they degrade the budget process to a mere forecasting exercise of exogenous developments; failures to predict these correctly then become the first step to losing control over spending and deficits.

Where non-decisions prevail strongly and are considered part of a country's culture of government, the government budget becomes heavily dependent on institutions outside the annual budget process, i.e. wage-setting institutions in the public sector, the social security system, the welfare system and labour market regulations. Non-sustainability of public finances may then be caused by weaknesses in these areas.[39] The implication for EMU is that an assessment of the sustainability of public finances will often include an assessment of these institutions, and demands for institutional reform may include demands for reforms in these areas. The European Council recognized this principle when it asked Italy to reform its pension system as a pre-condition to enter EMU. Next, we illustrate the point by reviewing Germany's experience in the 1980s.

Institutional reform may include demands for reform in areas outside the budget process, such as wage-setting institutions.

Following the second oil shock, Germany experienced a fast decline of its economy. The government's fiscal expansion negotiated at the G7 summit in Bonn in 1978 contributed further to the deterioration of its fiscal performance. The SPD-led coalition finally broke down in autumn 1982, when the smaller partner, the Liberal party, rejected Chancellor Schmidt's policy as short-sighted and inconsistent (Hellwig and Neumann, 1987: 113).

A new coalition government of the Liberal Democrats and the Christian Democrats assumed power, promising to consolidate public finances and to address the mounting unemployment problem. In line with the supply-side arguments proposed by the Bundesbank and the Council of Economic Advisors, the fiscal consolidation was expected to lower interest rates, stimulate investment and, thus, help to overcome the unemployment problem. Moreover, the new government intended to improve the performance of the labour market particularly for young people, through active labour-market policies and deregulation (CDU, 1983).

During its first years in office, the new government focused its activities on the consolidation of the budget. Table 4.3 summarizes the fiscal consolidation. The primary deficit was quickly reduced, and the reduction was achieved on the correct side of the budget, reversing the previous increase in government spending. At the more disaggregate level, the table reveals that the fiscal expansion under the Schmidt government was mainly due to rising public purchases and an increasing

Table 4.3 The German fiscal adjustment in the 1980s – effect and composition

	1977 (1)	1981 (2)	1985 (3)	Difference (2)–(1)	Difference (3)–(2)
Debt	27.3	35.4	41.7	8.1	6.3
Balance	−2.4	−3.7	−1.2	−1.3	2.5
Revenues	45.3	45.3	46.0	0.0	0.7
Expenditures	47.7	48.9	47.2	1.2	−1.7
Transfers	21.1	21.1	20.3	0.0	−0.8
Wages	11.0	11.3	10.6	0.3	−0.7
Purchases	8.1	8.8	8.7	0.7	−0.1
Investment	3.3	3.2	2.4	−0.1	−0.8
Interest payments	1.7	2.3	3.0	0.6	0.7
Primary balance	−0.7	−1.4	1.9	−0.7	3.3

Source: European Commission (1997b)

government wage bill, while the consolidation focused mainly on transfers. After 1985, the consolidation lost force and the deficit was allowed to increase slightly again. As a result, the government failed to stabilize the debt ratio effectively.

Nevertheless, Table 4.3 indicates that the broad symptoms at least were healed successfully. The government, however, remained remarkably inactive regarding labour-market reforms. New programmes of labour-market management, including training programmes and new rules for early retirement, were started (OECD Economic Survey – Germany, 1985). Efforts to deregulate the labour market and make it more flexible remained patchwork and half-hearted, however.[40] As a result, the government's labour-market policy did not achieve the promised reduction in unemployment. Instead, the unemployment rate increased from 4.5% in 1981 to 8.0% in 1985, and even in the subsequent period of strong real-growth it declined merely by 1.8% until 1990. In particular, the prevailing rigidities in the labour market did not allow a reduction in long-term unemployment, the share of which in total unemployment increased from 42% in 1983 to 48% in 1985 and remained at that level until 1990.

The failure to remedy the weaknesses of labour-market institutions in the 1980s is important to understand in our context, because it positioned Germany very badly for coping with unification. The immediate extension of West Germany's labour-market institutions to the East German economy in 1990 is the key to explaining the collapse of East Germany's economy in the 1990s and the subsequent fiscal disaster for the federal government.[41]

The unification process and the restructuring of the East German economy led to a renewed increase of the unemployment rate which reached 10.3% in 1996. In 1995, the share of long-term unemployed resumed again the pre-unification level. The government's response was similar to its policy in the early 1980s: massive training and public works programmes, subsidized work-places and early retirement were the central elements (see OECD Economic Survey – Germany, 1996). These responses left the structural problems unchanged, and instead increased spending pressures. The deterioration of Germany's budgetary position described in Section 3.3 was the result. Efforts to improve the institutions, which finally began in 1993 (OECD Economic Survey – Germany, 1994), remained patchwork. Only recently, some more significant steps towards a more flexible labour market were taken (OECD Economic Survey – Germany, 1997).

In summary, Germany's experience contains an important lesson for the sustainability of public finances. Even if the symptoms of a deficit problem are recognized and corrected, it is important that the underlying causes are identified and addressed. Of course, German unification in itself posed an unprecedented fiscal problem for the German government, but the failure to address the institutional problems more effectively in the 1980s has no doubt made the fiscal consequences of unification more severe and last longer in the 1990s.

5

Assessing sustainability: a practical proposal

We now assemble all the pieces of the analysis and draw our conclusions by advancing a set of concrete criteria to evaluate the public finances of a European Union member state. Above, we have argued that a workable concept of sustainability should capture the controllability of fiscal policy. Emphasizing controllability, a measure of sustainability should centre around four critical elements:

- a focus on the controllability of fiscal flows and the deficit;
- a disaggregate view of the composition of government spending and revenues to detect the symptoms of non-sustainability;
- attention to institutional failures causing non-sustainability;
- the use of measures and constraints that are relatively easy and uncontroversial in the implementation.

The purpose of this chapter is to put these elements together and to derive a tool for guiding the assessment of a country's public finances.

In doing so, we face a number of trade-offs. First, a realistic and practical assessment of sustainability must recognize a fundamental difference between what can be done immediately and what needs more time. As we have argued above, the institutional sources of non-sustainability are not easy to pinpoint unambiguously; they take time to correct, and they often involve sensitive political and institutional issues. Sovereign governments usually do not want to be perceived as negotiating institutional and constitutional issues with other governments. On the other hand, policy-makers do need a measure of sustainability that is readily and clearly implementable in the short run, for two specific purposes: (i) aiding the political decision about EMU membership; (ii) after EMU membership has been decided, for an early detection of loss of control over spending and deficits, so as to facilitate an effective monitoring of problem situations.

Thus, we propose an approach that integrates quantitative and qualitative information and uses it at different points of the assessment process. For the more immediate assessment of public finances, we need an indicator of sustainability that is readily available and unambiguously measurable. Such an indicator will necessarily focus on the symptoms of non-sustainability. For the more long-run perspective, we need information that is mainly focused on the institutional sources of the problem. Such information will necessarily be less easily quantifiable, more controversial and more open to negotiations.

5.1 Monitoring the process of regaining sustainability

Our approach adopts the logic of the Maastricht Treaty in that the sustainability of a country's public finances will not be questioned as long as it meets the double standards of the 3% deficit ratio and the 60% debt ratio. While these numbers are, of course, subject to debate and may, at a later point, be changed in the Treaty, the rule we follow is that there is a set of well-defined conditions under which the sustainability of a country's public finances will simply be assumed as a matter of principle, with no further measurement or questions asked.

Once these conditions are violated, however, the benign presumption ceases. Thus, the practical question is: given that a country has violated the double standards, under what circumstances can it be regarded as moving in the right direction, and under what conditions should its public finances be regarded as sustainable again? The focus is, thus, on the process of regaining sustainability.

Violating the benign presumption.

Starting from the violation of the double standards, we divide the process of regaining sustainability into five stages, summarized in Box 5.1.

■ **Stage 0**: Obviously, the first question must be, 'Has the deficit moved back towards the 3% criterion and the debt ratio towards the 60% limit in the year(s) following the

Moving in the right direction.

initial violation of the double standards?' Following the criteria of the Maastricht Treaty, we ask this question with regard to the total deficit. Another question is whether the actual or the cyclically-adjusted deficit should be considered. In principle, the cyclically adjusted deficit is preferable; however, the well known practical problem is that it lends itself to manipulations. As a compromise on might use the cyclically adjusted deficit, provided that the cyclical adjustment is done by the OECD as an non-partisan organization in the process – as opposed to the country in question – and the reference year is the previous year, rather than some elusive measure of potential or trend GDP. Otherwise we prefer the actual deficit, and we use that below.

Obviously a fall in the deficit from 5% to 4.9% of GDP would hardly qualify as an encouraging move. A minimum reduction in the deficit ratio of, say, 0.5% of GDP should be imposed. If this is not met, there is no visible movement back to sustainability, and the country is considered remaining in stage 0. If it is, we conclude that a consolidation has begun and the next stage can be considered.

The $\frac{2}{3}$ Rule.

■ **Stage 1**: The question here is, 'Has the adjustment occurred on the right side of the budget?' As we argued above, experience suggests that expenditure cuts should be in line with the expenditure increases that caused the deficit in the first place, and symmetrically for revenue increases. Since interest expenditures can hardly be changed by policy actions in the short run, we focus on primary expenditures and the primary deficit at this stage. More specifically, suppose that expenditure increases contributed x% to the increase in the primary deficit before the consolidation. Then, for the country to pass stage 1, the share of spending cuts in the reduction in the primary deficit during the consolidation should be at least αx%, where α is a constant between 0 and 1 to be agreed upon in advance. Our evidence of successful adjustments in Chapter 2 suggests that α should be $\frac{2}{3}$. In the next subsection, we provide a simple formula that can be applied at this stage. If the criterion is not met, the country remains in stage 1, if it is, the next stage is entered.

Disaggregation of spending and revenues.

■ **Stage 2**: This stage extends the approach of stage 1 to the individual components of primary expenditure and revenues. The critical question here is whether steps have been taken to reverse the increase in the spending item or the shortfall in the revenue category primarily causing the deficit to rise. To implement this stage in practice, the same formula could be used as in stage 1, this time applied to individual components of the expenditure and revenue sides.

To keep the assessment of fiscal policy at this stage manageable, a realistic breakdown could be as follows: on the expenditure side, capital expenditures, transfers to households, wage expenditures, non-wage consumption and other expenditures; on the revenue side, direct taxes on households plus social security contributions paid by employees, direct taxes on business plus social security contributions paid by employers and indirect taxes. This breakdown has the advantage that it follows closely the convention adopted by international organizations like the OECD and EUROSTAT, and it is therefore readily available, even on a cyclically-adjusted basis, with minimal delays. If the resulting criteria are met at this stage, assuring that the problem is being attacked at the source, the country can then move to stage 3.

■ **Stage 3**: The focus now shifts to the institutional deficiencies causing the loss of sustainability. Here, we ask whether or not the government has taken measures to identify the institutional weakness and exposed it to sufficient public scrutiny and attention to produce significant changes in the behaviour of the decision-makers involved, albeit changes of informal nature. In practice, bringing institutional weaknesses to public attention often helps to remedy the problem itself. If so, the country moves to stage 4.

Institutional Reform.

■ **Stage 4**: Here, the focus is on visible and formal institutional change to rectify decision-making practices that have been identified as the sources of excessive spending or a shortfall of revenues.

Our hierarchy ends here. Note that the five stages must not necessarily be thought of as following each other over time. In practice, identifying institutional problems may precede or come simultaneously with the required changes in spending and revenues. The different types of information needed, however, make it preferable to separate these stages.

BOX 5.1   Regaining sustainability

Stage 0   *Has the deficit moved back towards the 3% criterion and the debt ratio towards the 60% limit?*

If no significant movement back to sustainability has been achieved, the country is considered remaining in stage 0. If yes, the next stage can be considered.

Stage 1   *What is the relative contribution of spending cuts and tax increases to the consolidation?*

For the country to pass stage 1, the share of spending cuts and revenue increases in the reduction of the deficit during the consolidation should be at least x% of their initial contribution to the fiscal deterioration. Our evidence on successful adjustment in Table 2.3 suggests that x should be at least $\frac{2}{3}$.

Stage 2   *Have steps have been taken to reverse the increase in the spending item or the shortfall in the revenue category primarily causing the deficit to rise?*

Here, the focus is not the total of each resource flow but individual components of the expenditure and revenue sides. If the problem is being attacked at the source, the process can then move to stage 3.

Stage 3   *Has the government taken measures to identify the institutional weakness and exposed it to sufficient public scrutiny and attention to produce significant changes?*

The focus now shifts to the institutional deficiencies causing the loss of controllability. If the government seriously tries to detect the institutional weaknesses and initiate changes, the next stage can be considered.

Stage 4   *Has the government actually changed the underlying institutional sources of the fiscal problem?*

Countries changing the relevant institutions and budgeting practices of policy-makers pursue a very thorough reform. They have moved furthest in the process of regaining controllability.

At which stage should the EMU be satisfied and declare the country's public finances sustainable again?

Given this structure, the most critical question obviously is this, 'Once a country has violated the double standards and is moving through the stages of regaining sustainability, at which stage should the EMU be satisfied and declare the country's public finances sustainable again?'

From our earlier analysis, it is easier to judge what is *not* sufficient than what is sufficient. Clearly, a country should not be considered having regained sustainability, if it remains in stages 0 or 1. Note that this is independent of the 3% and the

60% criteria! As long as the symptoms of the problems leading to a state of non-sustainability have not even been recognized and addressed, the risk of the government losing control over public finances remains, and the benign presumption should not be re-invoked.

Although the same points can be made about stage 2, we recognize that this stage requires more refined and detailed calculations that are, by their nature, more likely to be controversial. As it is usually the case, it is easier to ask a country to reduce its expenditure by a certain fraction of GDP, than to make specific requests on which expenditure item to cut and by how much. However, although one might feel, in view of these difficulties, that a country's public finances should be declared sustainable again if it moves successfully to stage 2, this would clearly be inappropriate. It would imply that governments could get away with never addressing the more detailed symptoms, let alone the sources of their earlier fiscal problems. Curing merely the gross symptoms leaves little hope that the underlying problems have been solved. Thus, we strongly advocate that a country's public finances should not be declared sustainable again before it leaves stage 2 successfully.

A country's public finances should not be declared sustainable again before it leaves stage 2 successfully.

Judgement about institutional deficiencies causing deficit problems and their appropriate remedies are obviously still more controversial and must rely more strongly on qualitative criteria than the assessment made up to stage 2. A practical question regarding these stages is what type of information could be used in the assessment of a country's institutions and where to find it. Fortunately, international organizations, and the OECD in particular, have developed a strong tradition in monitoring economic and social policy institutions in the member countries. Since the OECD is not an interested party in the EMU, this provides a good point to start. Obviously, EU and national organizations can be asked to provide further information. In stage 3, the existence of government reports to parliament about the relevant institutional problems can be regarded as adequate evidence. In the end, however, one must realistically recognize that the assessments at stages 3 and 4 involve difficult and delicate judgements, which cannot be made with the same precision as those regarding the symptoms of non-sustainability.

While a strict application of our analysis implies that a country should only be considered as having regained sustainability after moving successfully through stages 3 and 4, the preceding

Information about institutional improvements can be used to reach a more qualified assessment of a country's situation in stage 2.

considerations imply that such a judgement would be politically difficult and may be impossible in practice. In the end, therefore, a more practical approach would be to use information about institutional improvements to reach a more qualified assessment of a country's situation in stage 2. That is, a smaller cure of the symptoms may be accepted as sufficient to declare sustainability, if it comes with evidence of appropriate institutional reform. An example would be the British case in the early 1980s, where not enough was done initially to contain the growth of transfer payments – the source of the rising deficit – but the decision-making processes were improved by introducing the Star Chamber and putting the public expenditure survey on a cash basis. In contrast, even a cure of the symptoms that seems sufficient at face value may be regarded as not enough, if there is no evidence for an institutional reform that is clearly deemed necessary to make the fiscal consolidation last.

It is clear from these considerations that our proposal does not amount to a toughening of the double standards. Instead of tightening the constraints on the aggregate fiscal deficit, it tries to guide the assessment by using additional information. All experience indicates that this is a more promising approach to secure lasting fiscal consolidations than imposing ever tighter limits on the deficit.

5.2 A numerical gauge for the symptoms

For stages 1 and 2, numerical criteria for the deficit and the components of the budget are needed to provide objective, easily measurable and highly visible criteria. This can be implemented practically in the following way. We begin by breaking the budget into x components. At stage 1, $x = 2$, i.e. the budget is broken down into expenditures and revenues. At stage 2, x is larger than that.

Let E denote the expenditure ratio and D the deficit ratio, all relative to GDP and cyclically adjusted. Let t be the current year, and T be the year in which the fiscal adjustment started, i.e. the year the cyclically adjusted deficit started falling sufficiently.[42] Finally, let τ be the year in which the fiscal expansion started, i.e. spending or the deficit started to grow relative to GDP. To avoid practical difficulties, we will neglect an annual improvement in the deficit before year T if it reduced the deficit ratio by less than $\frac{1}{2}$% of GDP.

To let a country move from stage 1 to stage 2, we require that:

$$\frac{E_t - E_T}{D_t - D_T} \geqslant \alpha \frac{E_T - E_\tau}{D_T - D_\tau}$$

where, in view of the empirical evidence, we set $\alpha = \frac{2}{3}$. In words, our criterion requires that the contribution of expenditure cuts to the deficit reduction between T and t should be at least two thirds of the contribution of expenditures to the build-up of the original problem between years τ and T.

As mentioned above, for stage 2 the criterion would apply to a more refined breakdown of the budget, i.e. on individual expenditure and revenue items. At the more disaggregated stage, practical implementability requires a smaller α, say, $\alpha = \frac{1}{2}$.

In Tables 5.1(a) and 5.1(b), we apply these criteria to the three cases studied in Section 3.3, Germany, France and Sweden. The tables indicate that Germany remains a stage 0, since its deficit did not show a sufficient decline by 1996. France moved to stage 1, but remained there, since it failed to show sufficient action on the expenditures side, where the deficit started. Sweden finally moves through stage 2, and, given the country's institutional improvements discussed in Chapter 4, would pass the two further stages, too.

Table 5.1(b) forcefully illustrates why Germany's deficit problem was not solved. Transfers, the main source of increased spending in the emergence of the deficit problem, were allowed to increase further during the attempted stabilization. Wages and public investment, which both contributed less to the rising deficit, saw the largest adjustments on the spending side. Partly as a result of Germany's weak labour-market performance, direct taxes fell during the attempted stabilization. Thus, as a typical example of an unsuccessful consolidation, Germany's stabilization in the 1990s failed for not attacking the problem at the source.

Table 5.1(a) Adjustments and change in public deficits

	Beginning of consolidation	Change in deficit ratio to 1996	Comment
France	1994	−1.5	pass stage 0
Germany	1993	0.3	remain in stage 0
Sweden	1993	−8.7	pass stage 0

Note: See tables in Section 3.3 for data sources.

Table 5.1(b) Contributions to fiscal deterioration and adjustments in the 1990s

| | Contribution (in percent of change in deficit) to | | | |
| | Deterioration | Adjustment | | Comments |
		Actual	Required	
France	**(1989–94)**	**(1995–6)**		remain in stage 1
Revenues	−9	82	0	
Primary spending	109	18	72	
Germany	**(1992–3)**	**(1994–6)**		remain in stage 0
Revenues	−67	−800	0	
Primary spending	167	1000	111	
Sweden	**(1989–3)**	**(1994–6)**		pass stage 1
Revenues	30	24	20	
Primary spending	70	76	47	
France	**(1989–94)**	**(1995–6)**		remain in stage 1
Transfers	74	−18	37	
Consumption	40	6	20	
Wages	26	−12	13	
Purchases	9	−100	4	
Investment	−6	12	0	
Germany	**(1992–3)**	**(1994–6)**		remain in stage 0
Transfers	200	−500	100	
Consumption	17	500	8	
Wages	33	600	17	
Purchases	−33	−200	0	
Investment	0	500	0	
Sweden	**(1989–93)**	**(1994–6)**		pass stage 2
Direct taxes	26	15	13	
Indirect taxes	4	3	2	
Social security contributions	5	9	2	
Transfers	44	25	22	
Consumption	11	23	6	
Wages	8	15	4	
Purchases	5	−10	2	
Investment	−8	−16	0	

Note: See tables in Section 3.3 for data sources. Numbers do not add up to 100% due to rounding errors in the data and missing spending or revenue categories.

Thus, our judgement about recent developments differs from the assessment of the Maastricht consolidation process given in a recent study of the European Commission (European Commission, 1997a). This study describes the recent consolidation efforts and notes that some European countries have achieved consolidation through spending cuts, others through revenue increases.[43] On this basis, it concludes that the Maastricht process has initiated a new path of public finances in the EU. The study, however, fails to take the final step of applying the principle of attacking the problem at the source. In the end, it only points out that there have been different patterns of deficit reduction with no clear standards of judging the underlying fiscal strategies. Our analysis and proposal in contrast emphasize that successful consolidation requires the right kind of adjustment.

6

Conclusions

As the convergence process towards EMU comes to an end and almost all EMU candidates will violate the double fiscal criteria, a practical interpretation of sustainability of public finances is needed to guide the assessment of the candidates' readiness for joining EMU and, even more importantly, for the continued assessment of their fiscal policies once EMU has begun. In this study we have proposed such a practicable approach. It rests on three main elements: a more disaggregate view of fiscal policy than that pursued in the Maastricht Treaty; the principle that fiscal problems must be attacked at the source to achieve a lasting consolidation; and the claim that non-sustainable public finances are ultimately caused by institutional weaknesses which, therefore, must be addressed to regain sustainability.

Our view of sustainability, and the process we propose in this study, radically departs from EU traditions in an important way. Until now, governments and the European Commission alike have regarded it inappropriate for the EU to interfere with the structure of a member state's fiscal policies and the institutions shaping it. The reason is that changing the composition of public spending and revenues, and reforming institutions, touches on sensitive domestic political interests, and these should be left to the country itself. Does the EMU have a right to make demands in these regards?

Our answer to this important question is quite simple. All empirical evidence and experience points to the fact that successful fiscal consolidations require adjustments in the structure of government expenditures and taxation, and these often demand institutional reforms to make the improvements last. Thus, if one is convinced that sustainability of public finances is an important condition for the success of EMU, the Union will rightfully have to address the member states' fiscal policies at a deeper level than just the aggregate deficit.

Notes

1. For example, see Eichengreen and von Hagen (1996) for a discussion.

2. Brandner, Diebalek and Schuberth (1997) use the HP-Filter to decompose the budgetary data into a trend and a cyclical component.

3. For a discussion of different techniques and the problems associated with the HP-Filter see Baxter and King (1995) and St-Amant and van Norden (1997).

4. We should add that measures of the sustainability of fiscal policy tend to be highly correlated with the current fiscal surpluses (see for instance Buiter, Corsetti and Roubini (1993)). This is not particularly surprising, if one thinks of how these measures are constructed, but it emphasizes once more that, in practice, what really matters is, to a large extent, the flow of government net liabilities.

5. See von Hagen (1992), von Hagen and Harden (1994, 1996), Kontopoulos and Perotti (1997), Velasco (1997).

6. This subsection applies a variant of the methodology introduced in Alesina and Perotti (1995) and (1997), who also first drew attention to the empirical regularities discussed in this subsection.

7. Belessiotis (1995) comes to a similar conclusion based on Granger causality tests for several EU member states.

8. See Alesina and Perotti (1995, 1997) for a sensitivity analysis.

9. See IMF (1996b), OECD (1996), Heylen (1997).

10. In 1973/74 expenditures jumped from 35.4% to 43.3% and transfers from 12.3% to 16.4%, while the compensation of employees to GDP ratio slightly decreased by 0.1 percentage points. These amounts remained fairly stable until the end of the decade, the most significant development being the slow decrease of transfers to 14.8% in 1979.

11. It is worth a mention that the previous government came to fall, because the parliament did not approve its budget (OECD *Economic Survey* – Ireland, 1982).

12. According to de Haan *et al.* (1992: 94) government employment declined from 314,000 to 307,000 between 1982 and 1984.

13. The government did, however, declare a Programme 'Building on Reality', which foresaw the reduction of the deficit (OECD *Economic Survey* – Ireland, 1985: 27).

14. The government increased the revenue share through higher taxes on wealth, inheritances, gifts, natural resources, tobacco and beverages and a higher VAT rate (OECD *Economic Survey* – Sweden, 1985: 57–8).

15. The successful containment of wages rested on wage ceiling negotiated with unions and a substantial reduction in public employment in 1985/86 from 1413 million in 1985 to 1406 million in 1986 (OECD *Economic Survey* – Sweden, 1985: 70; OECD *National Account Statistics*).

16. Higher tax rates were enacted on alcoholic beverages and tobacco, oil and petroleum and on hotel services and product groups. The capital tax rose and politicians decided upon temporary measures, such as a levy on forced savings in 1989/90 (OECD *Economic Survey* – Sweden, 1989: 97, 98; 1991: 116, 118).

17. Net capital transfers turned negative in 1987 due to a levy on pension funds and insurance companies. Moreover, interest payments dropped 2.4 percentage points between 1986 and 1990 (European Commission 1997b; OECD *Economic Survey*, 1987: 65).

18. Economic growth declined drastically between 1979 and 1981, private investment fell by cumulative 16 percentage points in 1980/81 and unemployment more than doubled from 1979 to 1982 rising from 4.0% to 9.7% (OECD *Economic Outlook*, 1997).

19. Though the 10% was not achieved, substantial reductions in the number of employees occurred, so that it remained under the 1980-level until 1988 (Rajah and Smith, 1994: 288).

20. Instead of using the greater of price or wage increases in the indexation formula, only the price could be used. This measure yielded almost 20% lower pensions for a married person in 1988 (Rajah and Smith, 1994: 287).

21. Nonetheless, the primary balance maintained an average surplus of 1.4% in 1983–5.

22. The goal of expenditure reduction was superseded in 1984 by the aim of holding spending at its current level and in 1986 replaced by the requirement that total public spending should decline as percentage of GDP, even without privatization proceeds (von Hagen and Harden, 1995: 396).

23. See Cabral (1996).

24. Computed from European Commission (1996a: Table 7a).

25. The structural balance improved from −7.6% in 1986 to −0.6% in 1987 and remained above −2% afterwards, with the exception of 1990 (OECD *Economic Outlook*, 1997).

26. The Irish consolidation presents a turning-point in the country's recent history. The orientation toward budget discipline still prevails in the 1990s (see Cabral, 1996 and European Commission, 1996b).

27. The following is based on OECD *Economic Survey* – France, (1995: 31–7; 1997: 45–9) and IMF (1995: 5–13).

28. See among others OECD *Economic Survey* – Germany, (1993, 1994), Bundesministerium der Finanzen (1994).

29. For a description and an analysis of the crisis see IMF (1996a) and Lindbeck *et al.* (1994).

30. A major part of the overall expenditure increase can be attributed to state support for major Swedish banks (Giavazzi and Pagano 1995: 20; OECD *Economic Survey* – Sweden, 1995: 28).

31. See Weingast *et al.* (1981) for the classical exposition of the argument.

32. Italy's experience with growing welfare payments is a prime example for this mechanism. In the past 30 years, Italian politicians used the disability pension system quite openly to buy voter support. See *New York Times*, Sept. 19, 1997.

33. See Velasco (1997), von Hagen and Harden (1995).

34. See von Hagen and Harden (1996) for a formal discussion of the two approaches.

35. Austria's and Finland's debt ratios increased after 1992, but these countries were not bound by the Convergence Programme.

36. The first reason why this is so is that delegation creates a principal agent problem that becomes relevant, if the members of the executive have very different views about the spending priorities. In a coalition government, it would be difficult to vest the finance minister with important strategic powers, because the finance minister necessarily has to come from one of the coalition parties, and the other parties would have to fear that the finance minister would abuse his power to assure that his party gets a larger share of the tax money than justified by the coalition agreement. Furthermore, the finance minister in a single-party government can threaten defecting spending ministers more strongly than in a coalition government, since a minister can be dismissed from the executive without disturbing the stability of the government. This threat can be backed up by the support of the prime minister, whose position is stronger in a single-party government than in a coalition. Contracting, in contrast, is the proper approach for coalition governments. The most important threat to assure enforcement here is the threat to break up the coalition; this is also why the legislature must be more powerful to scrutinize the executive under this approach. In a single-party government, in

contrast, threatening the death of the current government is not an effective enforcement mechanism: nothing will happen, if the ruling executive decides to walk away from the fiscal targets it set for itself.

37. The odd case in this table is Germany. To understand this case, it is important to realize that Germany's proportional representation system is augmented by a minimum vote requirement: parties winning less than 5% of the votes do not obtain any seat in parliament. As a result of this, post-war German governments have typically been two-party coalitions of one large and one small party (the Liberal Democrats). In this situation, neither coalition partner could threaten effectively to break up the coalition, since neither one would easily find an alternative partner for a new coalition. The ineffectiveness of the threat implies that the contracting approach does not work, making Germany a delegation state instead.

38. See Weaver (1986) for the related non-formal discussion.

39. For example, employment-protection legislation and worker bargaining power may contribute to higher unemployment which undermines the revenue base and puts additional spending pressures on the budget; see Scarpetta (1996) for empirical evidence.

40. See Jacobi *et al.* (1995) and Hellwig and Neumann (1987) for details.

41. See for example, Sinn and Sinn (1992) and von Hagen (1998). While observers outside Germany often argue that the collapse of East Germany's economy was caused by an excessive 'exchange rate' of East Germany's currency for Deutsche mark, German observers today agree that excessive wage demands that turned into relatively generous unemployment compensation and kept East German workers from moving to West Germany were by far more important. For a noticeable exception see Hallett *et al.* (1996).

42. To assess when the deficit starts increasing and when it starts falling, recall that we ignore small reductions of less than 0.5% of GDP. We propose to do the same to identify the year when the deficit started to increase.

43. Note that some of the classifications in the European Commission's study are subject to change if the timing of the consolidation is changed. For example, the Belgian adjustment is classified as entirely revenue-based in the period 1992–6, while a broader picture would recognize the caps and targets on spending imposed by Belgian governments after 1990.

Bibliography

Alesina, A., Hausmann, R., Hommes, R. and Stein, E. (1995), *Budget Institutions and Fiscal Performance in Latin America*, mimeo.

Alberto, A. and Perotti, R. (1995), 'Fiscal Adjustment: Fiscal Expansions and Adjustments in OECD Countries', *Economic Policy* 21, pp. 207–48.

Alberto, A. and Perotti, R. (1997), 'Fiscal Adjustment in OECD Countries: Composition and Macroeconomic Effects', *IMF Staff Papers* 44 (2), pp. 210–48.

Baxter, M. and King, R.G. (1995), 'Measuring Business Cycles: Approximate Band-Pass Filters For Economic Time Series', *NBER Working Paper* No. 5022.

Belessiotis, T. (1995), 'Fiscal Revenues and Expenditure in the Community', *Economic Papers* No. 114.

Blanchard, O., Chouraqi, J., Hagemann, R.P. and Sartor, N. (1990), 'The Sustainability of Fiscal Policy: New Answers to an Old Question', *OECD-Economic-Studies* 15, pp. 7–36.

Brandner, P., Diebalek, L. and Schuberth, H. (1997), *Structural Budget Deficits and the Sustainability of Fiscal Positions in the European Union*, Vienna, Osterreichische Nationalbank, mimeo.

Buiter, W., Corsetti, G. and Roubini, N. (1993), 'Excessive Deficits: Sense and Nonsense in the Treaty of Maastricht', *Economic Policy* 16, pp. 57–100.

Bundesministerium der Finanzen (1994), *Finanzbericht*, Bonn, BMF.

Cabral, A.J. (1996), 'Facing Similar Budgetary Problems, the Response in Ireland, Italy and Belgium' *Bulletin de Documentation* 56 (2), pp. 1–30.

Christdemokratische Union (CDU) (1983), *Wahlprogramm 1983 – Arbeit, Frieden, Zukunft: Miteinander schaffen wir's*, Bonn, mimeo.

de Haan, J., Sterks, C.G.M. and de Kam, C.A. (1992), 'Towards Budget Discipline: An Economic Assessment of the Possibilities for Reducing National Deficits in the Run-Up to EMU', *Economic Papers* No. 99.

de Haan, J. and Sturm, J. (1994), 'Political and Institutional Determinants of Fiscal Policy in the European Community', *Public Choice* 80, pp. 157–72.

de Haan, J., Moesen, W. and Volkerink, B. (1997), *Budgetary Procedures: Aspects and Changes – New Evidence for Some European Countries*, Paper presented at the NBER/ZEI Conference on 'Budgetary Institutions and Fiscal Policy', June 1997.

Edwards, P., Hall, M., Hyman, R., Marginson, P., Sisson, K., Waddington, J. and Winchester, D. (1995), 'Great Britain: Still Muddling Through', in Ferner, A. and Hyman, R. (eds), *Industrial Relations in the New Europe*, Oxford, Blackwell Publishers, pp. 1–68.

Eichengreen, B. and von Hagen, J. (1996), 'Fiscal Policy and Monetary Union: Federalism, Fiscal Restrictions, and the No-Bailout Rule', in Horst Siebert (ed.) *Monetary Policy in an Integrated World Economy – Symposium 1995*, Tübingen, Mohr, pp. 212–31.

European Commission (1996a), '1996 Broad Economic Policy Guidelines', *European Economy* No. 62.

European Commission (1996b), 'The Economic and Financial Situation in Ireland. Ireland in the Transition to EMU', *European Economy – Reports and Studies* No. 1.

European Commission (1997a), 'Economic Policy EMU – Part B Specific Topics', *Economic Papers* No. 125.

European Commission (1997b), *Statistical Annex of the European Economy*, Brussels, European Commission.

General Accounting Office (GAO) (1994), *Deficit Reduction – Experiences of Other Nations*, Washington D C, General Accounting Office.

Giavazzi, F. and Pagano, M. (1995), 'Non-Keynesian Effects of Fiscal Policy Changes: International Evidence and the Swedish Experience', *CEPR Working Paper* No. 1284.

Hahm, S.D., Kamlet, M.S. and Mowery, D.C. (1994), *The Political Economy of Deficit Spending in Nine Industrialized Parliamentary Democracies: The Role of Fiscal Institutions*, mimeo.

Hallerberg, M. and von Hagen, J. (1997a), *Electoral Institutions, Cabinet Negotiations, and Budget Deficits in the European Union*, Paper presented at the NBER/ZEI Conference on 'Budgetary Institutions and Fiscal Policy', June 1997.

Hallerberg, M. and von Hagen, J. (1997b), *Electoral Systems and Government Deficits*, mimeo.

Hallett, H.A., Ma, Y. and Mélitz, J. (1996), 'Unification and the Policy Predicament in Germany', *Economic Modelling* 13, pp. 519–44.

Hellwig, M. and Neumann, M.J.M. (1987), 'Economic Policy in Germany: Was There a Turnaround?', *Economic Policy* 5, pp. 105–45.

Heylen, F. (1997), 'A Contribution to the Empirical Analysis of the Effects of Fiscal Consolidations: Explanation of Failure in Europe in the 1990s', *University of Gent Working Paper* 97/32.

International Monetary Fund (1995), *France – Recent Economic Developments*, Washington D C, IMF.

International Monetary Fund (1996a), *Sweden – Selected Issues*, Washington D C, IMF.

International Monetary Fund (1996b), *World Economic Outlook*, Washington D C, IMF.

Jacobi, O., Keller, B. and Müller Jentsch, W. (1995), 'Germany: Co-determining the Future', in Ferner, A. and Hyman, R. (eds) *Industrial Relations in the New Europe*, Oxford, Blackwell Publishers, pp. 218–69.

Kontopoulos, Y. and Perotti, R. (1997), *Fragmented Fiscal Policy*, Paper presented at the NBER/ZEI Conference on 'Budgetary Institutions and Fiscal Policy', June 1997.

Lindbeck, A., Molander, P., Persson, T., Petersson, O., Sanmo, A., Swedenborg, B. and Thygesen, N. (1994), *Turning Sweden Around*, Cambridge, MA and London, MIT Press.

Milesi-Ferretti, G. (1997), 'Fiscal Rules and the Budget Process', *CEPR Discussion Papers* No. 1664.

Molander, P. (1995), *Re-evaluating the Swedish Budget Process – 1996*, Swedish Ministry of Finance, mimeo.

Organisation of Economic Co-operation and Development (1995–7), *OECD Economic Outlook*, Paris, OECD.

Organisation of Economic Co-operation and Development (1983, 1984, 1986), *OECD Economic Survey – Denmark*, Paris, OECD.

Organisation of Economic Co-operation and Development (1995), *OECD Economic Survey – France*, Paris, OECD.

Organisation of Economic Co-operation and Development (various years), *OECD Economic Survey – Germany*, Paris, OECD.

Organisation of Economic Co-operation and Development (various years), *OECD Economic Survey – Ireland*, Paris, OECD.

Organisation of Economic Co-operation and Development (various years), *OECD Economic Survey – Sweden*, Paris, OECD.

Organisation of Economic Co-operation and Development (1983), *OECD Economic Survey – United Kingdom*, Paris, OECD.

Organisation of Economic Co-operation and Development (1994), *Employment Outlook*, Paris, OECD.

Organisation of Economic Co-operation and Development (on diskette), *OECD National Account Statistics*, Paris, OECD.

Pierson, P. (1996) 'The New Politics of the Welfare State', *World Politics* 48 (2), pp. 143–79.

PUMA (1994), *Public Service Pay Determination and Pay Systems in OECD Countries*, Paris, OECD.

Rajah, N. and Smith, S. (1994), 'Fiscal Developments in the United Kingdom since 1980', *European Economy – Reports and Studies* No. 3, pp. 281–307.

Sargent, T. and Wallace, N. (1981), 'Some Unpleasant Monetarist Arithmetic', in Miller, P-J. (ed.) (1994), *The Rational Expectations Revolution: Readings From the Front Line*, Cambridge, MA and London, MIT Press, pp. 103–29.

Scarpetta, S. (1996), 'Assessing the Role of Labour Market Policies and Institutional Settings on Unemployment: A Cross-Country Study', *OECD Economic Studies* 26, pp. 43–98.

Sinn, G. and Sinn, H.W. (1992), *Jump-start: The Economic Unification of Germany*, Cambridge, MA and London, MIT Press.

St-Amant, P. and van Norden, S. (1997), 'Measurement of the Output Gap: A Discussion of Recent Research at the Bank of Canada', *Bank of Canada – Technical Report* No. 79.

Stein, E., Talvi, E. and Grisanti, A. (1997), *Institutional Arrangements and Fiscal Performance: The Latin American Experience*, Paper presented at the NBER/ZEI Conference on 'Budgetary Institutions and Fiscal Policy', June 1997.

Strauch, R. (1997), *Budget Processes and Fiscal Discipline: Evidence from the U.S. States*, mimeo.

Velasco, A. (1997), *A Model of Endogenous Fiscal Deficits and Delayed Fiscal Reforms*, Paper presented at the NBER/ZEI Conference on 'Budgetary Institutions and Fiscal Policy', June 1997.

von Hagen, J. (1992), 'Budgeting Procedures an Fiscal Performance in the European Communities', *Economic Papers* No. 96.

von Hagen, J. (1997), *European Experience with Fiscal Initiatives: Fiscal Institutions, Maastricht Guidelines, and EMU*, mimeo.

von Hagen, J. (1998), 'East Germany: The Economics of Kinship', in P. Desai (ed.), *The Integration of Transforming Economics into the World Economy*, Cambridge, MA and London, MIT Press.

von Hagen, J. and Harden, I. (1994), 'National Budget Processes and Fiscal Performance', *European Economy – Reports and Studies* No. 3, pp. 311–418.

von Hagen, J. and Harden, I. (1995), *Budget Processes and Commitment to Fiscal Discipline*, mimeo.

von Hagen, J. and Harden, I. (1996), 'Budget Processes and Commitment to Fiscal Discipline', *IMF Working Paper* WP96/97.

Weaver, K. (1986), 'The Politics of Blame Avoidance', *Journal of Public Policy* 6 (4), pp. 371–98.

Weingast, B.R., Shepsle, K.A. and Johnson, C. (1981), 'The Political Economy of Benefits and Costs: A Neoclassical Approach to Distributive Politics, *Journal of Political Economy* 89(4), pp. 642–64.